FRANCIS POULENC

*To my granddaughter
Helen, whose talents
are such that she should,
when she enters her
teens in a few years' time,
vividly relish the music of
Francis Poulenc*

Oxford Studies of Composers

FRANCIS POULENC

WILFRID MELLERS

Oxford   New York
OXFORD UNIVERSITY PRESS

Oxford University Press, Walton Street, Oxford OX2 6DP
Oxford New York
Athens Auckland Bangkok Bombay
Calcutta Cape Town Dar es Salaam Delhi
Florence Hong Kong Istanbul Karachi
Kuala Lumpur Madras Madrid Melbourne
Mexico City Nairobi Paris Singapore
Taipei Tokyo Toronto
and associated companies in
Berlin Ibadan

Oxford is a trade mark of Oxford University Press

Published in the United States
by Oxford University Press Inc., New York

© Wilfrid Mellers 1993

First published 1993
New as Paperback 1995

British Library Cataloguing in Publication Data
Data available

Library of Congress Cataloging in Publication Data
Mellers, Wilfrid Howard, 1914–
Francis Poulenc / Wilfrid Mellers.
(Oxford studies of composers)
1. Poulenc, Francis, 1899–1963—Criticism and interpretation.
I. Title. II. Series.
ML410.P787M44 1995 780'.92—dc20 [B] 93-4412
ISBN 0-19-816338-X

1 3 5 7 9 10 8 6 4 2

Printed in Great Britain by
Biddles Ltd.
Guildford & King's Lynn

PREFACE

The standard biography of Poulenc, that by Henri Hell, is now regrettably out of print. The major recent study of him—*Francis Poulenc: His Artistic Development and Musical Style*, by Keith W. Daniel—was published in 1982 by UMI Research Press. This small volume, contributed to a series of studies of composers, cannot compete with, and barely refers to, the major works of Hell and Daniel. It rather attempts to discover Poulenc's heart by way of commentary on a number of works that seem to me to be not only representative, but also good. Although by the standards of a Koechlin or a Villa-Lobos Poulenc is not a prolific composer, he wrote far more music than could be encompassed in a book of this size. In concentrating on the better works I've not stressed critical 'placing': Poulenc's warts are not lingered over, for the writing of this book was an act of love. As I've grown old, this seems to me to be increasingly the main, if not the only, justification for writing about a creator and his or her creations. This is especially the case with an artist who works in a non-verbal language like music. Yet although love is apt to be submerged in a sea of technicalities, what one says about music cannot mean much if it is not backed by musical evidence. I have tried to maintain a balance between technical description and experiential interpretation, and hope that people sufficiently interested to read the book will refer to the scores of the pieces—such as *Les Biches, Aubade, Dialogues des Carmélites*, and the last three wind sonatas—that are discussed in some detail.

My main debt is to the collection of Poulenc's *Selected Correspondence* 1915–1963, superbly translated and meticulously edited by Sidney Buckland, and published by Gollancz in 1991. I have also made use of Poulenc's *Diary of My Songs*, published by Gollancz in the original French and in English translation by Winifred Radford, in 1985; of a volume of Poulenc's 'conversations' assembled by Stéphane Audel and translated by James Harding; and of Poulenc's affectionate book on Emmanuel Chabrier, published in English translation by Cynthia Jolly.

W.M.

Oliver Sheldon House, Aldwark, York
27 August 1992

v

ACKNOWLEDGEMENTS

The following extracts have been reproduced by permission of Editions Max Eschig, Paris: *Le Bestiaire*, No. 1, 'Le Dromadaire', bars 11–14 (Ex. 1), and No. 6, 'La Carpe', bars 9–11 (Ex. 2); *Cocardes*, No. 3, 'Enfant de troupe', bars 9–12 (Ex. 3); *Montparnasse*, bars 31–4 (Ex. 22); *La Courte Paille*, No. 3, 'La Reine de Cœur', bars 1–5 (Ex. 56), and No. 7, 'Lune d'avril', bars 20–30 (Ex. 57).

Heugel SA, Montrouge, have kindly given permission for the following to be used: *Les Biches*, vocal score, p. 29, ll. 3–4 (Ex. 7) and p. 50, last line, piano reduction only (Ex. 8); *Pastourelle* for piano, p. 4, last 6 bars (Ex. 12); Nocturne no. 1, the end of the coda (Ex. 13), and Nocturne no. 2, p. 8, last line (Ex. 14).

Grateful thanks for permission to reproduce music examples are also due to Chester Music Ltd. (Examples 4–6 and 51–5), Editions Durand & Cie. (Examples 15, 17–20, and 23), Ricordi (Examples 29–41), and Editions Salabert (Examples 9–11, 16, 21, 24–8, and 42–50).

CONTENTS

Every postman's little boy at the Lycée knew that as civilization went France was the cat's whiskers. Yes, that hyper-civilization, the glory of arts and letters. Versailles . . . At the same time, war after war—wilful wars, brutishness, oppression, injustice, *la misère* . . . And in the intervals of murdering each other, they listened to Lully and Rameau, and painted bread and fruit as Chardin did . . . made delicate objects, and cultivated that glow of sanity and balance in daily life . . . Able to wound, able to heal. How did one connect those spurts *à la lanterne*, of heroism, endurance, the reeling between the excesses of revolution and bureaucracy, the intellectual rigour and the rhetorical platitudes, the elegance, the arrogance, the exquisite domestic sensuality, *le petit train-train de la vie*, and all the niceness and avarice that went with it?

(Sybille Bedford, *Jigsaw: An Unsentimental Education*, a biographical novel, 1989)

Perhaps I will always be le Jongleur de Notre-Dame.

(Francis Poulenc, letter to Pierre Bernac, 1952)

LIST OF MUSIC EXAMPLES

PRELUDE

Après la guerre: Poulenc, Ricardo Viñes, et Erik Satie

The conventional view of Poulenc used to be that he was froth in the wake of the First World War: a witty boy-hedonist who, in the giddy 1920s, tweaked the noses of moribund establishmentarians. Since he has proved unexpectedly durable—more so than any of his colleagues among Les Six, including those who developed delusions of grandeur—we have had to eat our words; even his adolescent works no longer seem what they used to seem.

The Poulenc family came from the Auvergne, and had interests stretching into the Mediterranean basin. Francis's immediate predecessors were pharmaceutical engineers, living in some affluence. Born in 1899, at the end of the Old Century, Francis was educated at the Lycée Condorcet and as a boy enjoyed a plenitude of silver spoons. Books, visual arts, and music abounded in his home. His mother was a talented pianist who encouraged her son's musical aptitudes; her tastes, those of a well-to-do Frenchwoman, were inherited by her son, who relished Mozart, Chopin, Schumann, Scarlatti, Couperin, perhaps Grieg, rather than Beethoven and Brahms; nor did he spurn his mother's partiality for 'adorable mauvaise musique' like Rubinstein's notorious *Melody in F*. Mother also sided with her son in resisting the attempts of an academic woman friend to steer Francis into 'serious' pursuits at Vincent d'Indy's Schola Cantorum. She even preferred his toying with the avant-gardisms of Debussy and Ravel, Stravinsky and Schoenberg, to subservience to respectable convention. Perhaps there was affinity of spirit as well as kin between Francis's mother and his uncle Papoum, an *habitué* of French theatre and café-concert. These tastes the boy also shared, not merely in childhood, but throughout his creative life.

Since Francis was musically precocious, his mother decided that she should pass him over as a piano pupil to a teacher with greater expertise than herself. Who more appropriate than the Catalan pianist Ricardo Viñes, who was not only resident in Paris, but had become a leading advocate of modern Parisian music?

Although a player of unusual distinction in the classical repertory, Viñes owed his celebrity to his exploration of the new pianistic techniques—mostly a matter of colour and timbre—necessary to perform the piano music of Debussy and Ravel, and of their minor acolytes such as Déodat de Séverac and Federico Mompou who, coming from Languedoc and Catalonia respectively, were near-compatriots of the pianist. But Viñes's pioneering pianism was not restricted to impressionist-affiliated music; he also acted as propagandist for Satie and Stravinsky, and in general espoused the cause of the avant-garde. Unsurprisingly, Viñes cultivated the boy Poulenc as a protégé—especially after Francis, aged 18, had complained to Paul Vidal about his contemptuous rejection by the director of the Paris Conservatoire. ('Your music stinks, it is nothing but a load of balls. Are you trying to make a fool of me? Ah, I see you have joined the gang of Stravinsky, Satie, & Co. Well, then, I'll say goodbye.') This splenetic outburst was occasioned by Francis's *Rapsodie nègre*, composed at the instigation of Ricardo Viñes: with whose support Poulenc had no need of the establishment, for the pianist led him not only into the corridors of fashion but also into the wellsprings of feeling that had made fashion fashionable. Most important of all, Viñes introduced Poulenc to Erik Satie, perhaps intuitively realizing the interdependence of the relatively old composer and the very young one. Since the distinctive qualities of Poulenc's early music are dependent on the affinity between the two men it is necessary, before examining Poulenc's music in depth, to enquire why Satie, apparently a marginal figure, was then so seminal to modern music.

A mere fifty years ago Satie was regarded, if at all, as a blagueur who wrote funny sentences on his scores, wore pince-nez, reputedly never opened letters, and collected umbrellas, dustily stored in his dowdy apartment in the suburb of Arcueil. Nowadays, his reputation as a mini-master of historical as well as intrinsic significance is undisputed, while bits of his music are familiar to thousands who have never heard his name. That some of his early pieces now serve as musical wallpaper, hopefully promoting sales on TV commercials, is an irony that seems far from arbitrary. Satie's ghost must relish the joke; he—who invented 'musique d'ameublement'—has the last laugh, as well as the first.

Characteristically, Satie started with a dual identity: as a hermetically private Artist garbed in velvet jacket and floppy hat, and as a functional pop musician earning his exiguous daily bread in a Parisian café-concert. In both roles he reacted against old Europe's egomania: specifically against Wagner, whose *Tristan* and *Parsifal* had brought the wheel of humanism full circle, seeking quasi-religious ecstasy from the identification of love and death; and against Debussy who, dealing in *Pelléas et Mélisande* with the same theme, substituted for ecstasy a tender but tough fortitude. But what, in this twilight of humanism, was an artist to do if he wasn't, like Wagner, heroic or bumptious enough to offer his inner life as surrogate for the destiny of man nor yet, like Debussy, brave enough to accept the impermanence of the senses as the only truth humanly apprehensible? He must try neither to dominate through the assertion of will, nor passively to submit to the flux of feeling. If human experience failed him, he must seek the logic of geometry.

In the first phase of his career, contemporary with *Pelléas*, Satie sought to reintegrate the fragmented materials of tradition by juxtaposing splinters of melody and broken chord sequences, without obvious relation to one another or to development. The diatonic and chromatic harmonies in his 'Rose-Croix' works of the 1890s (made for a church with only one member, himself) are Wagnerian and Debussyan: but differ from Wagner in that they neither achieve nor seek climax, and from Debussy in that their directionless oscillations accompany melodic lines that are clearly defined and cleanly shaped. These modal melodies have their roots in plainsong, and perhaps to a degree in oriental cantillation—with no mystical implications, but simply because religious chant is linear, non-harmonic, impersonal, and ritualistic. Satie's *Messe des pauvres* of 1895, scored for organ with intermittent unisonal voices, is a poor man's mass in a strict and oddly touching sense. The hypnotically repeated, often pentatonic, melodic fragments suggest devotional liturgy, while the rootless harmonies induce a sensuousness now forlornly disembodied. Nor do the songs and dances Satie composed around the same time for his café-concert inhabit a totally different world. Being related to Parisian vaudeville, they show more respect for harmonic consequence; yet the tunes themselves—even in a number (like 'Je te veux') with unabashedly erotic words—have a meticulous chastity of line, so that a love-dance instils in us not so much Baudelaire's 'luxe et volupté' as his timeless and placeless 'calme'.

In these early works the verbal irony that Satie sometimes

xiii

introduced into his directives is self-protective. This remains true even when, having belatedly undertaken a course in strict counterpoint at the Schola Cantorum, he related his melodic–rhythmic pattern-making more to the figurations of classical European traditions, and to mechanistic clichés of popular music, than to liturgical chant. Since counterpoint and pop music could, no less than plainchant, be construed as non-subjective, there was no volte-face between Satie's first phase and his second. In the piano pieces of these years—roughly from 1908 to 1916—the juxtaposition of simple but unrelated conventions induces a sense of incongruity which, like the crazy logic of *Alice in Wonderland*, is the more telling for its self-consistency. Irony remains more verbal than musical. Child-like but not childish, Satie's music is unusually free of the detritus of sentiment, and of memory and desire—and therefore of past and future. Its 'presentness' explains its appeal to avant-garde artists of his own time, as well as to us today.

Cubism was a rallying-cry, in the visual arts, during those war and post-war years; and it is patent that Satie's reintegration of splintered fragments of the past has something in common with a cubist painter's search for geometric logic within a visible world wherein 'meaning' had floundered and foundered. Both shore fragments of Europe's past against our ruins, as Eliot put it in his seminal *Waste Land* of 1921; and it was not fortuitous that when, in his middle years, Satie attained fame it was as a composer of ballet: an art in which the order of gestural movement was, though a dream of beauty and grace, opposed to romanic introspection. Satie's *Parade*, described as a 'ballet cubiste', is a ritual as sophisticatedly self-conscious as any twentieth-century ritual must needs be. Created for Diaghilev and first performed in May 1917, it assembled a galaxy of talents, among whom Satie as composer proved equal to Cocteau as inventor of the mimed parable about the confrontation between men and machines, to Massine as choreographer, and even to Picasso as designer of the décor and costumes. Astonishingly enough, the gestation of *Parade* coincided in date with the horrendous apex to the First World War. Cocteau himself, *Parade*'s inventor, had direct experience of the Somme as an ambulance driver; and when he referred to *Parade* as 'the greatest battle of the war', he was not thinking of the frenetic squabbles between artistic collaborators, nor of the riots occasioned by the performance. He was rather expressing his sense of wonder that so precisely elegant an artefact should have been created from conditions that were so physically and morally appalling. This is why *Parade* remains a keywork of our century.

Nor is it surprising that, despite the vivacity of Picasso's visual images and the brisk precision of much of Satie's music, *Parade* owes its durability to its gravity, even gloom. The action takes place not in, but outside, a fair: into which four Managers are trying to lure the public (us). The characters who hope to sell their wares—the mercantile metaphor is pointed—are dancers, acrobats, jugglers, trick-cyclists, and the like; the frailty of their modal and diatonic patterns complements the regularity of their rhythms. They tread their sundry tightropes precariously, emulating the flight of birds as they teeter over a small abyss. They strikingly anticipate the unheroes of Samuel Beckett, for whom the bicycle—as Marshall MacLuhan pointed out—is a symbol of specialist futility in an electronic age.

But if Satie's acrobatic and juggling lovers are victims of fate, so are the Managers who appear to be pulling the strings. More machine-like than human, the puppet-Managers are themselves cubist abstractions; and the identity of the drivers and the driven parallels the relationship between Pozzo and Lucky in Beckett's *Waiting for Godot*, written forty years later. Latent terror becomes patent when the elegantly nervous dance is punctured by the blast of a 32-foot stop on an electric organ. This creates a horrendous reverberation—for us, it might be an atom bomb—and leads to a recapitulation of the dancer's phrases in mirror-reversal, for one can't expect forward progression in a waste land. Terror is an appropriate response, for if the Managers don't manage anything, being themselves puppets, who or what is pulling *their* strings? So machine-gods and human beings dance together to a fierce orchestral tutti wherein the Managers' obsessively rotating theme is pierced by screeches on a police-car siren. The circus performers—pentatonic Chink, ragtimey American Girl, jittery jugglers, and anxious acrobats—flee the stage, rejected by us the people, while the Managers dance themselves into frenzy in their efforts to explain that the real show is still to take place, inside the booth. What is truth? as Pilate asked: though without the minatory venom Satie's music generates from tension between the Managers' nagging, self-enclosed theme and the orchestral hubbub. The ballet ends, with a return to the gravity—not irony—of the opening Chorale, on this note of misunderstanding. The wistfulness of Satie's circus performers, as of Picasso's clowns and harlequins, consists in the precision with which they keep going, even though there is no point in their actions beyond the ordered patterns they create. Again like Beckett's creatures, they 'might as well strike before the iron freezes', and before they surrender their humanity to a mechanistic, post-Cartesian world that would reduce them to inanimate objects. Satie modestly remarked 'j'ai composé un fond à certains bruits que Cocteau juge indispensables pour préciser l'atmosphère de ses personnages'.

In another context Satie said: 'Je suis venu au monde très jeune dans un temps très vieux'; and it was his *jeunesse* that provided him, as he waited for Godot, with a slight bulwark against decay, death, and the thingness of things. Death haunts his third-phase music, most deeply in the *drama symphonique, Socrate*, written in 1920, and scored for 'white' sopranos and small orchestra. Its patterned monotone recounts with no expressive melodic inflexions, let alone poignant harmonies, the tale of the Wise Man's trial and death, as narrated by Plato and translated into French by Victor Cousin. The cool symmetry of the modal, fourth- and fifth-pervaded music has minimal human background. The balanced phrases float in an empty room, the walls of which are built of parallel mirrors. Though a tiny world, it is self-reflected into infinity; and there is no music like it since never before had the artist felt so apathetic about—not antipathetic to—humanity as to make such a strange achievement feasible.

In the famous last scene the pulse remorselessly slows down as melodic, harmonic, and rhythmic vitality drain away. There is no irony in this frigid apotheosis of death, nor in Satie's third-phase music as a whole. True, his final ballet, *Relâche*, created in 1924 with Picabia, starts off as a joke, though it is hardly conducive to hilarity. The word 'relâche' means 'no performance', nor was there one on the opening night, so that in fact—not in pretence, as in *Parade*—the audience was denied the show. When the ballet *was* produced, a (perhaps blasphemous?) three days later, Satie's stage direction was 'Le rideau se lève sur un os'; and the pattern-making of the music-hall clichés was indeed skeletonic.

Yet even in his denials and negations Satie was forward-looking. The score of *Relâche* incorporated an 'entr'acte cinématographique' to a short film of René Clair, in which a hearse and coffin figure in surrealistic farce. Satie's music was a highly influential blueprint for a musical technique appropriate to the silent movie. Similarly, he invented, in his 'musique d'ameublement', a pre-juke-box Muzak which is anti-art in that it is meant to be not listened to; while in remarking that 'this work is utterly incomprehensible, even to me', or that 'experience is one of the forms of paralysis', he came close to a Cage's or Beckett's acceptance of purposelessness as a paradoxical purpose. Today's minimalists, some of whom are death-dedicated, were also philosophically prefigured by Satie, whose own minimalism was, however, as economical in duration as in tones. On the one occasion on which he offered a harbinger of the eternal-seeming repetitiousness of a Philip Glass it was overtly a joke: his *Vexations* is an 84-second piece which is to be repeated 840 times, thereby proving that 'boredom is mysterious and profound'.

Satie was a far more radical avant-gardist than Poulenc ever was. None the less, the reasons for Poulenc's durability—for the austerity beneath the frivolity of his early music—are inseparable from the fact that he, while still a boy, recognized as did no other Parisian composer what Satie's music was 'about'. The recognition was not conscious; Francis simply knew that Satie must be a father-figure to him and, even quite late in life, still asked himself what Satie would have done about any compositional problem that confronted him. The superficial influence of Satie on Poulenc is already evident in the young man's *succès de scandale*, *Rapsodie nègre*, composed in the spring of 1917. Early in the next year Poulenc produced a mini-song-cycle, *Le Bestiaire*, which reveals the heart, as distinct from the façade, of Satie's music, while at the same time being a small original masterpiece to which Poulenc remained faithful for the rest of his life.

I

POULENC ET LA JEUNESSE

1. Poulenc, Satie, Apollinaire, and Cocteau: Rapsodie nègre *(1917)*,
Le Bestiaire *(1918)*, Cocardes *(1919)*

After the violence of the First World War, the presumptively
child-like Negro became a cult-figure in Paris, as is already evident in the ragtime sections in Satie's *Parade*. In the same year,
1917, Poulenc produced, at Ricardo Viñes's suggestion, his *Rapsodie nègre*; by the early 1920s black American jazz bands had
taken Paris by storm, and some great jazz musicians (Sidney
Bechet) and some charismatic black entertainers (Josephine Baker)
were resident in the city. Poulenc's first success was not, however,
overtly jazzy, though it was initiated by the young man's discov-
ery in a second-hand bookshop of a slim volume of poems pur-
porting to be by a black Liberian writing in French. Poulenc takes
over the identity of the pretend-poet, Nakoko Kangourou, but the
text he uses in the one movement with words is not in French,
but in an invented language derived from the euphonious word
'Honolulu'. The whimsicality, even the farce, of the text suggests
that Poulenc is not aiming at a totemistic negritude, but is rather
indulging in an adolescent game, at once comic and pathetic.

The prelude consists of rudimentary organum in parallel
fourths and fifths—prophetic of the opening of Ravel's magical
childhood opera, *L'Enfant et les sortilèges* (1920–5), when the
'fallen' child disrupts the cosy kitchen with his small savagery.
The chant of Poulenc's savage is even more primitive, but less
heartfelt, being a metrically rigid wail down a tetrachord. The
instrumental sonorities are more suggestive of dulcet Bali than of
darkest Africa, but that the technique is gauche is part of its
appeal; its naïvety is its integrity—which is why the music still
tickles the fancy, if it does not stir the heart. The smart public at
the avant-garde concert put on by the singer Jane Bathori, on 17
December, was delighted with the *jeu d'esprit* which offered
promise of artistic fruition.

Nor was this long in coming, for in the spring of 1918 Poulenc
found himself, as a young soldier, stationed at Pont-sur-Seine.

Perhaps the threat of war helped him to concentrate on the heart of the matter, especially since he was still in thrall to the poet Apollinaire, whom he had met shortly after his encounter with Satie at the notorious première of *Parade*. Here was a potent meeting of minds, for Poulenc responded to the kinship between the dry acerbity and tender inconsequence of both Satie and Apollinaire, and knew that the word and the voice were his fundamental impulse to creation. Hearing Apollinaire read his verses was

a wonderful thing: I believe it is essential for a composer who does not want to betray his poet. The timbre of Apollinaire's voice is like that of his works, melancholy and joyful at the same time. This is why my Apollinaire songs must be sung without emphasizing the ludicrousness of certain phrases. *Le Bestiaire* is a most serious work.

It is indeed, this being a quality it shares with Satie's music, which displays so singular a purity of heart—and of line, harmony, and rhythm. Poulenc's *Bestiaire* songs resemble Satie in being wide-eyed, open-eared, diatonic, like children's runes that sometimes exhale a whiff of street, circus, and music-hall as they rotate in an eternal present, with a chaste, sad, even solemn effect.

The identity between Poulenc and his poet was recognized not only by the composer himself, but also by the painter Marie Laurencin, who was soon to design the décor and costumes for *Les Biches*, the ballet that made Poulenc famous as an established anti-Establishmentarian. Writing a fan letter to Francis in 1921, Laurencin refers to the 'singsong quality of these admirable quatrains . . . You would think you were hearing the voice of Guillaume Apollinaire himself reciting these very lines.' Ironically, Apollinaire died at the age of 38, in the year in which Poulenc musicked his verses. Originally, the poems had been designed as a verbal–visual collaboration with Picasso, but in the event between Apollinaire and Dufy. 'Poetry is by its nature the language of light', Apollinaire remarked in reference to the first poem in the series; and he associated his catalogue of creatures with the legend of Orpheus, who affirmed the artist's potential mastery over inchoate Nature. So philosophically religious a concept helped Poulenc to understand the impulses 'behind' his juvenile *Rapsodie nègre*, and to present the menagerie in Apollinaire's verses in the visionary and iconic spirit of a medieval bestiary. As Blake put it, 'My Spectre around me night and day | Like a wild beast guards my way'; this is why the mastery of these mini-songs, as compared with the unlicked charm of the *Rapsodie nègre*, is manifest.

Le Bestiaire was originally scored for voice with flute, clarinet, bassoon, and string quartet, employed in a manner at once unsentimentally acerbic and poetically evocative. Poulenc also made a version for voice and piano which works so well that it has virtually displaced the ensemble setting. Poulenc regretted the loss of his initial concept which used the same instrumentation as *Rapsodie nègre*, without the piano but with the addition of a bassoon. Fortunately, the piano version is such that, if one has heard the ensemble setting, one can recreate its sonorities in the mind's ear, probably because Poulenc's piano textures are, like Satie's, scrupulously linear.

Significantly, the verses of the first song, 'Le Dromadaire', are not really about the beast at all:

> Avec ses quatres dromadaires
> Don Pedro d'Alfaroubeira
> Courut le monde et l'admira.
> Il fit ce que je voudrais faire
> Si j'avais quatre dromadaires.

The hero is clearly no dromedary, but Don Pedro with his dreams, his adventurousness, even his vulgar curiosity: qualities deflated by the fact that most people don't possess one dromedary, let alone four. Poulenc's music portrays Don Pedro and his beasts with deft precision, in a swaying 2/4 pulse, 'très rhythmé, pesant'. Dissonant seventh chords emulate the dromedary's cumbrous lollop, while descending semiquaver quintuplets may be his ill-tempered grunts. The effect is not in the least comic; nor is the voice part, which starts with a three-note ululation, then proceeds up and down a plain diatonic scale, reinforced, in Satien style, with unrelated concords (see Example 1). The same music is repeated for the remaining words; but the strange little piano postlude, suddenly quick, changes the perspective with a glimpse over the horizon. Its E major bliss is a fleeting vision of the wonders one might, given a sufficiency of dromedaries, momentarily enjoy.

'La Chèvre du Thibet' is a love-song lasting a mere eight bars. The words compare the silken coat of the goat with the golden fleece that Jason pursued over the wide world, but counters Jason's epic aspiration with the modest assertion that the locks of

3

Example 1   *Le Bestiaire*: 'Le Dromadaire, p. 1, last line.

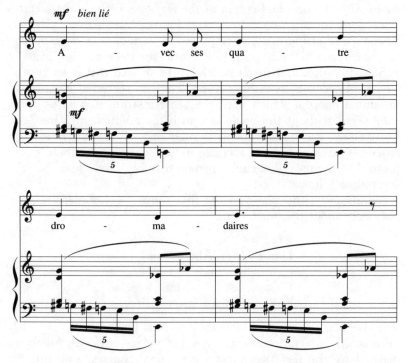

the poet's girl far outshine those of both goat and legendary hero. In a simple 4/4 pulse, the song is Satie-like in its linearity, its stepwise or pentatonic movement, and its metrical regularity. At the reference to questing Jason the piano part flowers in two bars embroidering a chord of the dominant thirteenth with grace-notes; but the last two bars about the girl's hair are naïvely pentatonic.

'La Sauterelle' is only four bars long, though these bars are 'lent', as well as paradoxically both 'souple' and 'sans nuances'. This grasshopper is a delicate creature who made food fit for St John. The poet hopes that his verses may likewise nourish superior people. Again, the vocal line sways gently, moving by seconds major or minor, or by pentatonic minor thirds. 'Les deux pédales' veil the sequential harmony, which floats seventh chords, decorated with 'grace' notes in more than one sense, over a gravely singing bass.

'Le Dauphin' presents the creature as an adventurer through uncharted seas—as in the first number Don Pedro and the poet had aspired to wander the wild world. The sea tastes bitter, and the poet's life is cruel; one shouldn't expect too much, even of a dolphin, as an icon. Poulenc's very Satiean music makes this audible in a two-bar phrase in 'innocent' A major, drily 'sans pédales' and, perhaps, without illusion. There's a hint of a street tune in the fourth-dominated vocal line. False relations between chords of A major and F sharp major hint at falsity, though Poulenc permits himself a brief wash of pedal and a slight rallentando in the last bar. The final A major chord glows with an added second.

Similarly ambivalent is 'L'Écrevisse', a crayfish who, like the poet and his love, moves 'à reculons'. Again the vocal line undulates with the tide, between major seconds and minor thirds. Although 'assez vif', this is not a happy song, its key being darkly seven-flatted A flat minor, with an unbroken tonic pedal. The voice ends by going 'backwards' in a groaning glissando from A flat to D flat, while the piano tumbles down an A flat minor scale, through an ostinato that sounds bitonal, though its double-flatted notation is—like the comparable passages in Satie—strictly grammatical.

'La Carpe', the final song, is the simplest and most profound:

> Dans vos viviers, dans vos étangs,
> Carpes que vous vivez longtemps!
> Est-ce que le mort vous oublie,
> Poissons de la mélancolie.

The regular 4/4 pulse, 'très triste, très lent', scarcely breathes. In the first bar the bass swings between tonic and dominant of deathly A flat minor, shifting to tonic and subdominant in the second bar; there's a watery demisemiquaver quiver, first through a minor, then a major, second, on each alternate beat. The vocal line, undulating between E flat and D flat, is also near immobility: which is why the first clause, when the line at last leaps through an octave, is so painfully affecting (see Example 2). The irony of those missing dromedaries of the first song proves to be endemic to the human condition. The carp, in their living death, are other than human in being beyond consciousness, and therefore 'beyond good and evil'. The timeless ticking of the clock stops only when dammed on the piano's viscous A flat minor triad, and allowed to vibrate as long as the sound lasts. It says much for the probity of the young Poulenc's awareness of modern man's alienation that he should have written this song two years before the final scene of Satie's *Socrate*.

5

Example 2   *Le Bestiaire*: 'La Carpe', p. 8, last line.

Also in 1918, Poulenc composed another song-cycle to verses by a poet with whom he was closely associated, though Jean Cocteau was not a Poulenc *alter ego* until, late in life, Francis set *La Voix humaine*, Cocteau's one-act play for one actress. The early Cocteau cycle, *Cocardes*, is not a heartfelt piece like *Le Bestiaire*, though it has documentary significance in so far as the surreal poems are exercises in popular style, illustrative of the thesis propounded in Cocteau's pamphlet, *Le Coq et l'Harlequin*. Its aesthetic was a protest against what Cocteau believed to be the self-indulgence of post-Wagnerian music and of high romantic art in general; but this protest functioned at a superficial level, compared with the iconic objectivity of Satie, and of Poulenc as his disciple in *Le Bestiaire*. According to Poulenc, both the poems and the music of *Cocardes* evoke 'Paris before 1914, Marseilles in 1918, and the Médrano Circus in 1920'. *Cocardes*, he adds, was the first of his 'œuvres de Nogent, avec une odeur de frites, d'accordéon, de parfum Pivier. En un mot tout ce que j'ai aimé à cet âge et que j'aime encore.'

6

If *Le Bestiaire* enshrines the spirit of Poulenc's childhood, *Cocardes* displays its flesh, for Nogent-sur-Marne is a village near Paris where Francis's grandparents had a country house, in which the boy spent many happy hours and days. The difference between the music of *Cocardes* and that of *Le Bestiaire* mirrors the difference between the Cocteau poems, which are snapshots or posters, and those of Apollinaire, which are iconic children's paintings. The two cycles offer the first instance of a pairing of opposites—a metaphysical chastity and physical sensuality—that will recur throughout Poulenc's music-making life. In *Cocardes* the link is not with the 'abstract' Satie of *Socrate* and the *Nocturnes*, but with Satie's 'musique foraine', which reached its apex two years later in the ballet *Mercure*, a collaboration with Picasso and Picabia. Poulenc also says that the songs were written under the orchestral influence of Stravinsky, in his fairground and peasant-band vein.

The first number, 'Miel de Narbonne', is a street scene with clowns, as vividly coloured as the poster-paintings of Roger de la Fresnaye, much relished by the young Poulenc. The song is longer than those in the *Bestiaire*, but only because it works on the collage principle, with abrupt intrusions of ferocity into suavity. The cleanly sculpted phrases are still Satiean, though without the aloof intensity of the Apollinaire songs. In this number the spell is broken by an unabashedly demotic polka; throughout, contrarieties of mood are accepted as though they were facts of nature. Cocteau maintained that irony would be inappropriate to verses that were a homage to the music-hall; though he added that the songs needed to be as good as Chabrier, and they are.

'Bonne d'enfant' is a hotchpotch of street impressions—the sounds and sights that affect and sometimes afflict us as we stroll in the afternoon sun. Great democratic absolutes like liberty, equality, and fraternity are debunked along with the ephemeral side-shows of a commercial world. The music is cheerily military, with fanfare-like dotted rhythms and sonorous tenths in the harmony; yet the effect is wistful as well as whimsical. The last song, 'Enfant de troupe', is the simplest, though not, like the final number of *Le Bestiaire*, the most profound, for it extrovertly offers a catalogue of childish delights—caramels, acid drops, pastilles, Hamburg beer, syrup of raspberries. Musically as well as verbally the song is kaleidoscopic, with alarming shifts in tempo and dynamics. Brief moments of tenderness mollify the music-hall

7

Example 3   *Cocardes*: 'Enfant de troupe', p. 9, first four bars of l. 3.

manner with Satiean grace-notes, but the piano's imitation-accordion leaves us in the grubby street (see Example 3). This kind of piano writing provides a transition to Poulenc's first works for his own instrument, the most famous of which, *Mouvements perpétuels*, was also composed in his first vintage year of 1918.

2. 'Perpetual Movement' in the Early Piano Works (1918–1920)

The title, *Mouvements perpétuels*, is a key to the work's nature, for each of the three pieces, in being based on a pre-ordained ostinato 'perpetually' repeated, rediscovers what Geza Roheim called the 'paradise of archetypes and repetition' within which so-called primitive peoples, including children, live, move, and have their being. Such an abrogation of adult responsibility is a relief we may call blessed. It is not restricted to 'savages' and children; for it resurfaces in black American jazz, in urban pop musics, and in the music of the minimalists that overlaps with pop. Since Poulenc's *Mouvements perpétuels* are in process but not progress, the music offers a continuum to live in, as nearly as possible free of intentions and ambitions. The throwaway inconclusions to all the pieces confirm this, in the same way as the day-before-yesterday's barrelhouse pianists, yesterday's blues and jazz pianists, and today's precariously surviving cocktail-lounge tinklers fade out on an unresolved flat seventh, or 'blue' note. It would be delightful, the fade-outs suggest, if this paradise of archetypes and repetition could, like a fairy-tale, go on 'for ever and ever'; it is sad, but touching, that we know it cannot.

No. 1, 'assez modéré' in speed, adheres unchangingly to its ostinato which, in one bar of 4/4, combines oscillating tonics and dominants with a rising and falling scale (see Example 4). The four-bar tune droops pentatonically, as though 'singing itself'; but the answering three-bar phrase melodically shifts to an undulating scale of C, while the ostinato remains in its initial B flat. The first two bars are repeated, but the second two are dissonantly mutated into the minor while the ostinato remains major. Bell-like major ninths resonate over the ostinato and the tune, repeated, is chromaticized and tickled with acciacaturas, similar to those in Satie's exotic *Gnossiennes*. All the music is recapitulated, 'sans nuances', and the piece dissipates in a five-bar coda: two bars of the original ditty, two in which the melody wavers between D and C, slowing down by way of its own weight, and a final very slow bar in which pitch and movement dissolve in pianissimo bitonality. Only in the final bar does the ostinato cease, chromaticized in unresolved appoggiaturas. Thus disembodied, the music's tranquillity, even its happiness (if that's what it ever was), sounds solitary, incipiently sad.

Example 4   *Mouvements perpétuels*, p. 2, first four bars.

En général, sans nuances

The second piece, also 'très modéré' in 4/4, has an ostinato of falling chromatics balanced by rising minor thirds or sixths. After six bars the ostinato becomes a widespread chord of the ninth, now without chromatics. The right hand's tune toys with rising fourth, major second, and repeated notes, until the 'très chanté' melody turns into a spread chord of the dominant thirteenth, 'legèrement timbré' by both pedals. Satie's jugglers from *Parade* would seem to be imminent; like them, the young Poulenc performs mini-miracles of poise and grace, keeping going, as best he may, in the face of pretty desperate odds. How fearful the odds is suggested in the two-bar coda. This hopefully restarts the original ostinato pattern, only to be effaced in a pianissimo glissando that slinks out off-key: the juggler drops his airborne balls or the acrobat topples off his too-tight rope.

The final piece looks as though it may be more assertive, and is certainly longer. Marked 'alerte', it is in pastoral F major, though it has a touch of the urban swagger of Satie's 'musique foraine'. The sturdy tenths in the left hand support a perky, stepwise-moving tune, but a beat drops out of the second clause, and a Satiean oompah passage, beginning fortissimo, soon fades. Tempo changes to 3/8 as ostinatos float through a G minor chord with added ninth and flat seventh. Another little miracle of grace floats, 'avec charme', over the decorated G minor triad; the long phrasing across the barlines leaves Satie's jugglers suspended in time and space. A return to the 'alerte' tune fails, however, to come off, dissipating into a slightly slower, pentatonic undulation: which trembles into trills and contrary motion scales, wispily fading on a dominant thirteenth (see Example 5). *Mouvements perpétuels* are uniquely magical, charming in more than one sense, and as impervious to fashion as are the age-old children's runes with which they are affiliated.

Another piano work, written in the same year of small wonders, 1918, is hardly less magical in effect, though it is less well-known than *Mouvements perpétuels*, probably because it is for piano duet. The work is a 'Sonate' only in the sense that it is sounded rather

Example 5   *Mouvements perpétuels*, p. 8, last line.

than sung, for it has no hint of sonata form or development. It opens (once more 'modéré' in 4/4) with a rhythmic ostinato on a C minor chord with added notes—a bell-sonority rather than harmony. Against the syncopated metre of the seconda part the prima dances a pentatonic motif with small chromatic flourishes. Suddenly 'très doux', an *enfantine*-like tune rings in high register, again recalling Satie's paradoxically calm but jittery acrobats. The rhythmic ostinato dissipates in trills; the prima part coos the pentatonic tune over a pedal D, with an inner chromatic line interlaced. Although there is a da capo of the original rhythmic ostinato in C minor, the piece is hardly an orthodox ternary structure, since the near-pentatonic tune is constant throughout. A coda-bar, marked 'strident', whisks the ostinato aside, with an effect which is slightly alarming, as well as risible.

The second movement, 'Rustique', is more child-like than bucolic. 'Naïf et lent', it is a 'white note' piece without a single accidental, perhaps indebted to Stravinksy's piano duet pieces of 1914–17. The dovetailed diatonic and pentatonic motives entwine in a smiling serenity that is never soporific. The end is a throwaway on, not in, the dominant; its gentle reiterations suggest both a nursery ditty and Balinese gamelan, with no need for the question mark we place over the last bars of the three *Mouvements perpétuels*. The finale is a children's dance-game rather than song; energy accumulates when the whiteness of C major is bitonally telescoped with E flat major. The tempo speeds to presto and, over drum-beats in the bottom reaches of the keyboard, a Phrygian variant of the original tune appears at first on C, then E, then G, the keys defining a major triad. The da capo is, as so often in Poulenc, curtailed, and after a repetition of the bitonal C major–E flat major passage, the scalic theme prances in Stravinskian major sevenths. The last two bars present the scale figure in Phrygian C minor, very softly, rounded off by a 1/4 bar that elides a C major triad with G flat as well as E flat major. We hear the multiple chord as C major with a plethora of blue notes.

Scarcely less delectable is the *Suite in C* for solo piano, written in 1920. All three movements distil luminosity from C major scales and flowing figurations recalling white-note Stravinsky in the quick sections, and Satie's 'enfantines' in the (not very) slow movement. But around this date Poulenc realized that he needed to spread his wings. He took lessons from Charles Koechlin, that great contrapuntist and apostle of French civilization, and tried himself out in the manners of relatively 'advanced' composers. The piano *Promenades* of 1921, for instance, flirt with the polyharmonies and luxuriant textures of Ravel, as well as with Stravinskian polytonality and polymetre. Temporarily, Poulenc's true self is obscured, though he never really wavered in his loyalty to his spiritual father, Satie. And a transition from Satie to Stravinsky made sense in terms of Poulenc's development, for Stravinsky was a major composer and an internationalist, by way of whom Francis might establish a more central position. If Satie was Poulenc's spiritual father, Stravinsky was his revered role-model. In a letter to Paul Collaer, written in 1921, Poulenc remarked that for Stravinsky 'craftsmanship is simply a way of refining,' whereas for our 'old stuffed-shirts it is a way of making something grand out of nothing'. A little later, Francis was being sharply intelligent, not fashionable, when he praised Stravinsky's Wind Octet for being 'magnificent, so sure and solid'.

3. Poulenc and Stravinsky: Early Works for Wind Instruments (1919–1923) and the Trio for oboe, bassoon, and piano (1926)

In his early youth, however, the model for Poulenc's pieces for wind instruments was not so much the great Octet as the Russian-tinged works (such as *Pribaoutki*) that Stravinsky composed during the war years, discovering in them links between the worlds of peasant and of child. But whereas Stravinsky tended to exploit contrasts of mood ironically, Poulenc followed Satie in making us laugh not in a satiric or parodistic spirit, but simply at the incongruities inherent in the everyday world. In the 1918 *Sonate* the two clarinet-pipers chortle like mountebanks at a Petrouchka-style fair in the quick movements, while in the slow movement they lament in peasant monotone. There are still traces of this Russian heritage in the *Sonate* for clarinet and bassoon of 1922, though this piece is more genially francophile. Apropos of this sonata Poulenc wrote a letter to Koechlin, thanking him for the benefit he had received from his lessons in counterpoint, and professing himself 'rather pleased' with this product of his studies. He ought to have been still more pleased with the *Sonate* for horn, trumpet, and trombone of the same year; for although this brass trio is briefly modest it is, like Stravinsky's *Octet*, splendidly 'sure and solid'. The melodic lines are cleanly diatonic; each has its own identity which dovetails with the others. In the first section the trumpet tootles G major fanfares; the horn moves more soberly in scales and oscillating thirds; while the trombone is appropriately more measured in gait. A slower middle section, in a cross between E flat and B flat major and C and G minor, weaves arpeggios for the horn and cantabile crotchets for the trombone, which also flirts skittishly with the trumpet's fanfares. Suddenly quick, in B flat major, the music breaks into a grotesque hocket, the beats truncated and dislocated (see Example 6). The comedy, being guileless, lends added zest to the shortened da capo of the G major allegro and imbues the slightly slower coda— ambiguously major–minor and with chromaticized trombone— with a quality at once grave and clownish.

The slow movement starts from a similar ambiguity, unsure whether it is in B flat major or minor. The repeated patterns of the trombone part and the chromatics and grace-notes in the upper parts sound faintly Russian, but the serenity of the textures

Example 6   Sonata for horn, trumpet, and trombone, p. 4, l. 3.

is very French, anticipatory of *Les Biches*, on which Francis was already at work. Characteristic and beautiful is the passage in which horn and trumpet sing cantabile over the trombone's syncopated accompaniment; and the music's positive direction is reinforced by the rondo finale, which is in D major, dominant of the first movement's G. Precision of rhythm and lucidity of articulation ensure that the music always 'sounds'. Many years later—indeed in 1962, the last year of Poulenc's life—his friend the composer Henri Sauguet wrote to tell Francis that he had just heard a performance of this little trio that 'retained an extraordinary fresh force and fantastic individuality'. Thirty years later, it still does. This music is tonic to ageing minds and senses.

The latest in date of Poulenc's early cycle of works for wind instruments introduces a new dimension in the form of a piano, which is both polyphonic and harmonic by nature. Inevitably, the music graduates from the linear concepts of wartime Satie and Stravinsky towards Stravinskian neo-classicism. In 1922–3 Stravinsky had composed the Wind Octet that had so impressed Poulenc, and was adventuring into balletic styles which related both to the high baroque and to the romantic fairy-tale ballets of Tchaikovsky. Poulenc's Trio for oboe, bassoon, and piano follows parallel paths and at moments even anticipates Stravinsky's grandly hieratic *Oedipus Rex*, finished in 1927.

A Stravinskian starkness is manifest in the quasi-Lullian overture that serves as introduction. Four-part writing for piano, in Aeolian A minor, launches a classically double-dotted theme on bassoon, answered by the oboe a semitone higher, in B flat minor. A dominant ninth cadence lands us back in A minor, with baroque roulades on the wind instruments more frivolous than heroic. These lead, in Stravinskian time-travelling, into a champagne-like presto in 'youthful' A major, tinged with minor. The style is rococo crossed with Offenbachian *opéra bouffe*, and there are intimations of sonata form in what might be a lyrical second subject, in more strenuous song-tunes in dark F minor, and in an amiable quasi-codetta theme in F major. But sonata is abandoned as the movement assumes a ternary form, with a middle section at half speed. The wind instruments entwine in Mozartian or Rossinian cantillation, albeit with recollections of the heroic introduction. Gluck, that catalyst between baroque and rococo, is the presiding spirit, and is not effaced by the da capo of the A major presto, since this is too brief to re-establish itself.

The point of this emerges in the slow movement, which is melodically vocal in idiom and pianistically luxuriant. The key is B flat major; the gentle 4/8 tune relishes operatic turns; the piano purrs in arpeggiated triads. Soon the first movement's link with Gluck becomes patent, since his famous Orphic music in the Elysian Fields is interlaced with Poulenc's own themes, and becomes the main melodic drift of the movement. These delectable Elysian Fields are welcomed as a never-never land fusing present with past—only for the disparity between reality and illusion to render Poulenc a shade desperate. By the end of the movement the delights of pastoral F major have been, in a coda, shadowed with chromatics, and the final chord is in F minor, that key of *chants lugubres* and of the infernal regions that were reputedly contiguous to the Elysian Fields.

The dubiety of mood that Poulenc brings to this music, along with his 'time-travelling', makes him almost a post-modernist. Certainly the sequential harmony of the piano mollifies the woodwinds' linearity with incipient romanticism; the sharp sonorities, though not abandoned, are cushioned on and cosseted by dreams. But the rondo finale tries to make do with a healthy hedonism, being a bouncy gigue in D flat major, lower mediant to the F major–minor the slow movement had ended in, upper mediant (enharmonically) to the first movement's A major. The first triadic tune capers to the dominant, but the rondo episodes are pluralistic in embracing many contrarious moods. When Poulenc abandons a key signature, the frisky modulations hint at development, though this has more to do with high spirits than with incipient drama. Francis is content to be directionless (he wrote the piece in his beloved Cannes), and inconsequence is an aspect of his pluralism. The movement has affinities with a baroque French gigue, with an Offenbachian gallop in the lurid footlights of a Second Empire theatre, and—in the tight, Stravinskian coda—with the acerbity of post-war Paris. Oboe and bassoon have dual identities as Gluckian opera singers and as Satiean balletic clowns. This trio thus points the way to the idiom of Poulenc's music of the 1930s, and immediately to his association with the theatre: whence came his European fame.

2
POULENC ET LE RÊVE PASTORAL

1. The Diaghilev Ballet and Les Biches (1923)

The ballet that came to be called *Les Biches* was commissioned from the 22-year-old Poulenc by the great Diaghilev in 1921. Francis completed the score, in Poulenc country in Touraine, in 1923; and the piece was first performed at the Théâtre de Monte Carlo on 6 January 1924. Beginning on 26 May, further productions were staged at the Théâtre des Champs Elysées in Paris, as the ballet had been an instant success, for intrinsically musical and theatrical reasons. The French title literally means fawns, does, graceful young female creatures; but the word 'biche' was intended to contain a sexual *double entendre*, which the anglicization of the title to 'the House Party' neatly catches. Wit and spring-like fragrance ('naughty but nice') coexist in Poulenc's music, as they do in Marie Laurencin's décor and costumes.

Although the technical features Poulenc had acquired from Satie and Stravinsky are still evident in *Les Biches*, it is his first work that could never be mistaken for anyone else's. Indeed, his debt to Stravinsky is as much a matter of general concept as of musical particularities. Stravinsky had created for Diaghilev a balletic Rite of Spring set in the Old Russia, and had also made a ballet about a wedding among the Russian peasantry. Poulenc's *Les Biches* also celebrates a spring festival and a marriage— transported from White Russia to la Belle France, old and new. Stravinsky's still scarifying rite portrayed, in 1913, the sacrificial murder of a young girl and a potential rebirth: thereby paralleling the destruction of Europe during the first of the world wars, while at least offering hope—more positively explored in *Les Noces* of 1917—of renewal. The young Poulenc's ballet, composed early in the 1920s when peace was supposed to have broken out, renders both the spring rite and the wedding domestic, making them a simultaneous tribute to France's present and her past. For Poulenc made a 'ballet avec chœurs', quarrying the words and some of the tunes of the vocal episodes from 'chansons populaires françaises' of the sixteenth and seventeenth centuries. These verses and tunes are 'low' in provenance, courtship and wedding songs from village green and small-town market square. Poulenc's music, Nijinska's choreography, and Laurencin's décor and costumes translate them to a dream world that is eternal France, and at the same time the jazzy present. Stravinsky's sacrificial murder in *Le Sacre* and his orgiastic peasant-wedding in *Les Noces* had been real as aesthetic experience, while undoubtedly being games performed in the one case by a vast symphony orchestra (itself a product of industrial technology), and in the other case by an exotic percussion band with chorus. In both cases the instrumentalists were garbed in conventional concert uniform, while the dancers were masked in theatrical costumes. The audience included not one peasant; nor was a murder perpetrated, nor a wedding and bedding consummated. Poulenc makes a rite about courtship and marriage; sets it among young people in an Arcadia that might be called Monte Carlo; and reveals that his spring festival and rites of passage are what they always were—especially in the Old France of the Renaissance and of the Roi Soleil. Simultaneously, and affectingly, he explores the permanence and the impermanence of human institutions.

The overture evokes Old France; far from promising 1920s-style frivolity, it hints dolorously at medieval roots, in incantatory monody in lilting triplets on woodwind, with ambiguously major and minor thirds. The chant ends on a dominant of E minor, and the curtain rises on a 'general dance' in vivacious 6/8, in E major. Some of the traditional associations of E major—the sharpest major key in common use during the baroque era—with bliss, if not heaven, must be inherent in the music's ebullience, the more so since it aspires to the still sharper dominant. The aura is that of France's seventeenth and eighteenth centuries, but when young girls indulge in a fast French *valse* we are closer to nineteenth-century ballet. Incipient romanticism prompts a modulation to the minor and a chain of parallel ninths. Returning to 6/8, and moving to white C major, the music is 'strepitoso', with a repeated note tune that might be called 'low'. The fast French *valse* returns in the subdominant (A), followed by a truncated da capo in the tonic E. A chromaticized bridge passage refers to the 'antique' monodic overture; all this shilly-shallying of the 'giddy young things' in the contexts of history is slightly alarming in effect.

Even so, the next dance—after preludial ninth chords of

17

Stravinskian austerity—is a French rondeau apparently happy in the merry present. Its jaunty tune, based on an upward-thrusting scale leading to repeated notes, is in pastoral F major, in common time. The first phrase, tootled on trumpet, modulates sharpwards to the dominant, and is repeated. An answering phrase, accompanied by clinking parallel seconds, is also repeated, but in 'infernal' F minor—an event which will be consequential later in the ballet. For the moment, there is a sturdy cadence in the tonic minor, followed by the first rondeau episode, in F minor's relative, A flat major. The harmony is euphonious, with modulations to the (new) tonic minor and its upward mediant, C. This lyrical love-music, Gounodesque in romanticism, is linked to a second episode in 3/4, with ripely chromatic harmonies on six-part strings. This may be the incipient anxieties, rather than the fulfilled delights, of sexuality; the dance ends ambivalently, for after the trumpeted rondeau tune has returned to C and has modulated sharpwards to *its* dominant G, there is a sudden lurch back to F major—capped, moreover, by a coda in the tonic *minor*. There is no pretence that, even in Arcadia or Monte Carlo, love's course must needs run smooth.

Up to this point the guests at this elegant house party have danced and mimed, eschewing words. Now they embark on a 'chanson dansée', preceded by a slow introduction in Poulenc's antique manner, again placing the young things against the back-cloth of history. Three-part woodwind warble an incantation around fifths, sevenths, and ninths—a Stravinskian sonority that Poulenc has made his own. The dance-song itself is suddenly brisk, with fanfares percussively harmonized, and a vocal tune based on a simple D major triad. The men, using words from a seventeenth-century pop song, ask 'What is love?' and supply an answer: love is a cat who will entrap you if you don't watch out. A more cantabile, very feline, D minor phrase suggests that the boys might relish the pussy's assault; perhaps they encourage it in a recurrence of their bugle-blowing fanfares. A gentle episode in a modal D flat major and in caressingly syncopated rhythm flowers into choral ululations on 'Ah'. Insouciance again takes over as everyone indulges in a dance of 'les Chats et les Amours' together, back in F major, with a jolly tune over a singing bass.

Entrapment-by-cat occurs in the next dance, the deservedly famous Adagietto. In a letter to Diaghilev dated September 1922 Poulenc confessed that he had found the number troublesome:

how difficult it was! I hope I have avoided the 1830 waltz, the 1870 waltz, the Italian adagio, the 'wrong note' waltz à la Casella, and the sad waltz (*Parade*). In fact it is a dance in 2/4 time, very lithe, very *danceable*—and also andantino, beginning in B flat, then moving through the most unexpected modulations. I am sure this is what is required.

It was indeed: for the *amoroso* melody, lilting in semiquavers over a cantabile bass, combines triadic figures with sinuous chromatics, while being harmonized in sonorous sequential sevenths (see Example 7). Innocent in melodic symmetry, passively

Example 7   *Les Biches*: Adagietto, p. 29, ll. 3–4.

sensuous in harmony, the music is the essence of amorousness; and becomes even more so when, in an almost-grand peroration, the tune returns in the *sub*dominant, E flat. Tonal relaxation becomes an apotheosis, which can be followed by sequential sevenths *dolce e cantando*, as pussy purrs, claws sheathed. The dance ends with a distant revocation of the 'antique' monody, still in the subdominant, E flat.

The Adagietto is a dream of love; we are restored to fairly mundane reality by the next 'chanson dansée', pointedly called 'Jeux'. The words and tune, again of popular origin, are sung by men impersonating a father who has four marriageable daughters cluttering his house. The metre is fast, in 5/4 panning out to common time; the mode begins as Dorian on G. Father encourages his girls to marry any man who makes an offer, the sooner the better, though the daughters, entering off-key, evince slight enthusiasm, since 'J'aimerai que m'aimera'. There is something grotesque about this bucolic bargaining in a Monte Carlo theatre, but the effect, far from being ironic, makes us aware that the more things change, 'plus c'est la même chose'. What's going on in this house party is much the same as has happened throughout history in any French village or town. When the merry month of May is invoked the music dances in a sprightly vocalise, establishing kinship with Stravinsky's more primitive *Les Noces*, and with courtship rites through the ages. The boys and girls participate in 'choosing games' such as were played in remote antiquity, and are still played by real children. Excitement is generated by way of syncopated chromatics for the men, while the girls trill aloft. More seductively, the young men invite the girls home, and the young women invite the boys to 'faites-moi les yeux doux, et mettez-vous à genoux'. This abasement to the female principle prompts the most Satiean music in the ballet; nervous ostinatos induce a trance that is—understandably, in view of the mysteries that sex and love conceal—marked 'malincinico' (see Example 8). Magic is dismissed by a da capo of the original marriage-broker song, but the scene ends orgiastically in an accelerando climaxing on high Gs.

Poulenc described these 'Jeux', in a letter to Diaghilev, as 'a sort of hunting game, very Louis XIV'. This account serves, if we include low life as well as court vainglory in the reference to Louis XIV; but Poulenc points to a savage contrast, if not explicit irony, when he describes the succeeding Rag-Mazurka as 'terrify-

Example 8 *Les Biches*, p. 50, last line, piano reduction only.

ing'. Both the mazurka and its ragging are slow to emerge: for the movement opens with a literal quotation of the Rondeau's chromatic episode for six-part strings—music which, we suggested, may bear on the perils and perturbations of sexuality. At first the dance won't admit to these anxieties, for it begins in a skittish 3/8, in pastoral F major. But with a shift to 'lugubrious' F minor and with haverings between a 3/8 *valse* and a 6/8 Offenbachian gallop, Second Empire virility and vulgarity sweep us towards the present. Bit by bit we have moved from the 'green paradise of childish loves' that Ravel celebrated in the first and last of his *Chansons madécasses* to the glories of la Belle France, (which are simultaneously historical and mythical), and thence to the giddy present of Monte Carlo (manifest in the boogie rhythm of Franco-American jazz). Poulenc's rag borrows elements from Satie's famous rag in *Parade*, though it has more 'allure' than is typical of Satie's chaster muse. In the spirit of post-First-World-War jazz it is jittery and comically desperate, with none of Satie's latent gravity; incessant modulations, mostly through minor keys, enhance malaise, and a tango episode in B flat minor approaches the sinister. The climax, back in F minor, merits Poulenc's epithet 'terrifying'; and although aggression subsides into a da capo of the original bucolic dance in 3/8, the coda is formidably in F minor, swinging between tonics and dominants. A coda to the coda, marked 'un poco più calma', offers alleviation with a theme in the major, distantly derived from the 'dream of love' Adagietto; but a fortissimo rag-rhythmed cadence in F minor abruptly puts paid to that. Finally, a coda to the coda to the coda harks back to the 'antique' woodwind incantation, in three-part dissonant polyphony. The effect is not so much ironic as 'post-modernist', like the Elysian Fields episode in the trio for oboe, bassoon, and piano, to be written in a few years' time. How appropriate that *Les Biches* should have triumphed, in Paris, at the Théâtre des Champs Elysées!

The succeeding Andantino brings together the boys and girls, perhaps now men and women, and discounts the dizzy present in a gracious dance beginning in C major. Its themes are Mozartian rococo, related to, though not identical with, the themes of the Rondeau and the Adagietto. Gradually, overt quotations from the Adagietto intrude, and its feline sequential sevenths introduce the last statement of the C major tune. The coda dissolves in a haze of C major arpeggios with added notes, finally pierced by dissonant appoggiaturas, D flat to C. Perhaps this is an admission that the Adagietto *was* a dream, and a recognition of 'other modes of experience that may be possible'. In any case the final 'chanson dansée' sets the perilous present in the context of history. In a chant consistently modal in melody and antique in manners the boys offer the girls 'un joli laurier de France'. The young women reject this patriotically iconic tribute, effacing the men's Dorian B flat with a C major luminous in added seconds and sixths. More reluctant to relinquish dreams, they want *spring* flowers—'un bouquet de giroflées, tout frais cueilli'—rather than emblematic evergreens, and are presumably willing to accept the fact that freshly gathered flowers soon wither. The boys compromise on 'un collier de capucines . . . que j'ai couvert de baisers'. The kisses, if not the *capucines*, prove irresistible, and the key shifts to A major, traditional key of the burgeoning youth of men and maidens, and of the spring of the year. The music demonstrates that this consummation is not escapist: the harmony is toughened with parallel major sevenths and ninths, and the climax is rather grand, like a Frenchified *Les Noces*.

This is the end of the rite, though a finale is appended, beginning with frisky triplets in D major, then retrospectively reviewing themes of the ballet—including, among the love songs, the sinister rag, now spikily fragmented. The coda, returning to the triplet romp which is both rustic and Parisian, sends us home in sunshine, yet aware of shadows on the grass. The success of the ballet ('a triumph, eight curtain calls', according to Francis) must have been partly attributable to its being a mirror for its fashionable and wealthy first-night audience who could, if they would, spot themselves within Poulenc's and Laurencin's and Nijinska's half-lights and sexual obliquities. But that cannot explain why chic, of its nature ephemeral, proved so durable, and is still not threadbare. The strength of the piece lies in its existing at once within and without its time and place. Impermanence itself acquires permanence—as Stravinsky must have recognized when, in a congratulatory letter to Francis after the first performance, he remarked that 'you know the warm regard I have for what you are doing, and especially for *Les Biches*'. Marie Laurencin, having an 'interest' as the ballet's designer, acutely wrote to Poulenc: '*Les Biches moves* the Rich', adding that 'I am in no way responsible. Your music is'. The piece remained a high point in Poulenc's creative life, and holds its own alongside greater works like Stravinsky's *Le Sacre* and Satie's *Parade*. It has not dated, though fashion would seem to be its essence. Unsurprisingly, Poulenc created, in its wake, in the late 1920s, a few other works of vintage quality.

2. *Wanda Landowska,* Concert champêtre *(1928) and* Aubade *(1929)*

Les Biches had been commissioned by Diaghilev at the suggestion of the legendary Misia Sert, to whom Francis gratefully dedicated his ballet; it was thus born of the near-mythical 'beau mode', for the delectation of Beautiful People. The genesis of his *Concert champêtre* for harpsichord and small orchestra was more purely musical, for it was commissioned in 1928 by the formidable Wanda Landowska, who was no less impressed by Poulenc's precocious talents than Misia Sert had been. Nor was she impervious to his personal charm; and she fostered his music in the most practical way, by repeated performance. While *Concert champêtre* is a tribute to Landowska and to her instrument and while it contains conscious archaisms inspired by French harpsichord music, it is not a *divertissement à l'antique*. Like *Les Biches*, it exists simultaneously in past and present, and its 'scène champêtre' is not so much rustic as suburban. The music renders aurally 'incarnate' the Bois de Vincennes and Saint-Leu: lost Edens for Poulenc, where Couperin le Grand had a town house, where Rousseau and Diderot strolled and chatted, and where Landowska herself currently had a *pied-à-terre*. Moreover, the military motives that pervade the piece prove to be boyhood recollections of soldiers from a local barracks, drilling and bugle-blowing in the leafy squares. Present reality, memory, and dream are indivisible.

The slow introduction summons the glory that was Versailles. The orchestra, moving in a four-pulse in dotted rhythm, sounds processional, and is tonally ambiguous between D major and minor, with flat seventh. The harpsichord antiphonally exploits the same bitonality, with the help of mordents and appoggiaturas endemic to the instrument. But major tonality ousts minor; added seconds, fourths, and sevenths make for a nasal, metallic sonority comparable with neo-classic Stravinsky; and the introduction ends on, not in, the dominant. The main allegro is launched by solo harpsichord, with a tootling D major tune suggesting Couperin in his Commedia dell'Arte vein, supported by percussive dissonances in the left hand. When the orchestra thinly joins in, the 2/2 *moto perpetuo* modulates to the dominant, without generating a second subject; for this is another fairly substantial work constructed on the principle of collage. The *moto perpetuo* stops for an interlude of bugle-call fanfares on minor thirds, which the harpsichord intensifies with 'biting' mordents and chittering acciaccaturas. Regularly patterned figuration in continually volatile modulation creates a vulnerable equilibrium, again recalling Satie's acrobats. Climax occurs when the military motives grow assertive in sharp B major, jubilant on brass and timpani. The climax ends in riotous dissonance, followed by silence: out of which floats a harpsichord cadenza, paying deference to the 'free' preludial style of French harpsichord music. From a stepwise-moving monody in octaves the music time-travels to embrace Renaissance and even medieval sonorities within the realm of classical baroque. Modal mystery is swept away, however, by a da capo of the *moto perpetuo*, again introduced by the soloist. The final antiphony between soloist and orchestra, recalling the ceremonial introduction, is unexpectedly grim.

The slow movement is a Sicilienne, a pastoral dance to which Poulenc was addicted, perhaps for its sun-baked suavity. The G minor tune lilts on strings through a rising arpeggio and drooping scale; modulates to the dominant; then moves back to the tonic by way of a heart-easingly 'Neapolitan' A flat. The harpsichord starts with major–minor oscillations, but then embroiders the lovely tune with arpeggios. Tonality softens in the region of A flat and E flat majors, with ripely sequential sevenths, rendered 'doux et mélancolique' by chromatic alteration. The coda, oscillating between the orchestra's minor triads and the harpsichord's major-keyed arabesques, is at once romantically emotive and classically heroic.

Nor does the finale dispel ambiguity. The harpsichord opens 'très gai' in babbling D major triplets, again recalling Couperin at the Commedia dell'Arte. But the main orchestral tune, in 2/4, is 'low', especially when tickled by piccolo; and the Satiean 'musique foraine' is clownishly impudent when its fourths are inverted into sixths, and tonality sidesteps kaleidoscopically. Bugle-bands parade through suburban squares, climaxing in 'éclatant' brass fanfares in E flat, through which the falling thirds of the first movement intrude on horns (see Example 9). Ultimately these fanfares form the work's apex, for minor thirds in B major tie up with the ceremonial opening of the *Concert*.

The finale's coda, back in D major, begins with chattering harpsichord, allegro giocoso in 3/4. The orchestra answers antiphonally, with metrical dislocations to the stepwise-moving tune. Throughout the movement, which recurrently embraces oscillating minor thirds and heroic dotted rhythms, volatility of mood and manner makes for a vitality that disturbs. Poulenc's time-travelling and stylistic pluralism are not, like Stravinsky's, iconoclastic, but rather affirm that the totality of French civilization is still, for all the buffets it has suffered, alive and well in his musical metamorphoses. Up-to-the-minute audacities, the cosy conformities of yesteryear, and the panoply of French civilization from the Middle Ages, through the Renaissance, to the splendours of the Roi Soleil and the delectable decadence of the Second Empire, may be simultaneously present. The durable charm of *Concert champêtre* lies in the fact that we emerge from its mingle of merriment and melancholy not bewildered, but invigorated: uncertain of, yet ready for, whatever may happen next.

25

Example 9 *Concert champêtre*: Finale, p. 55, bottom line.

And in the next year, 1929, Poulenc rounded off the decade with a work closely related to *Concert champêtre*, and not inferior to it in quality. *Aubade* is a concert work for solo keyboard and small orchestra, while being also a theatre piece for a choreographed female dancer. It is not, like *Les Biches*, a full-scale ballet for theatrical performance, for it was commissioned by the Vicomte and Vicomtesse de Noailles for a ball in their Paris residence in the Place des États-Unis. Since Poulenc himself played the piano solo and Nijinska devised the choreography, the piece may be thought of as a private evolution from the public myth of the Diaghilev ballet: creating, in music and mime, images of order and grace to counteract the disorder and disgrace of 'the death of Europe', especially as manifest in the First World War. Indirectly, this is true even of Stravinsky's revocations of primitive savagery, since they are meticulously structured; it is patently true of Poulenc's *Les Biches*, which mutates rites of courtship into Marie Laurencin-like, tear-tinged bliss. In this context *Aubade* is a farewell to Eden, for the leading dancer represents Diane, goddess of chastity, a state which clearly doesn't agree with her. She is a beautiful young woman who might be one of those 'biches'; and the piece describes her frenzy as she runs away, certainly from sex, perhaps from love and life. Since Poulenc himself devised the scenario, it seems probable that this potentially tragic sequel to the ambivalent *Biches* had autobiographical undertones.

The first movement, Toccata, consists of a slow introduction and a *moto perpetuo*. The introduction sets the scene in antique, quasi-Greek style, with unisonal chant on brass, answered by piano. The modality, rooted on E, is pervaded by sharp fourths of what might be the Lydian mode on A, with a powerful but painful effect. Pain is not substantially diminished when brass gives way to woodwind in dissonant parallel fourths and sevenths. Beneath screeching trills on B, undulating sevenths are ambiguously major–minor, until the piano launches the allegro in a surging theme toughened with augmented seconds and Lydian fourths. The augmented seconds (C to D sharp) sometimes become identified with minor thirds (C to E flat), both in fierce false relation with the prevailing E naturals. Although the heroine has not yet appeared, the piano soloist (Poulenc) is her harbinger, in energy, rebellion, and incipient lunacy. Every bar modulates, as though trying to break from the prison of its perpetual motion: in this sense *Aubade*—a dawning, as its title indicates—is an attempted growing up from that preconscious 'paradise of archetypes and repetition'. Climax arrives in a wild metamorphosis of the toccata theme in dark F minor. Eventually, the music finds its way back to Aeolian A minor, the bass prancing through octaves and ninths, the figuration 'éclatant'. The final bars are suddenly, in deceptive triumph, in A major, that key of youth and hope!

There is point in the fact that the solo keyboard is not, as in *Concert champêtre*, a harpsichord, but a modern piano played by a modern composer, Poulenc himself, identified with the distraught 'biche' or goddess in that his toccata figuration defines her corporeal gestures. The curtain rises, on the A major chords that conclude the Toccata, to reveal a classical décor peopled by 'les compagnes de Diane', at 'le petit jour'. The music is in baroquely

Example 10 *Aubade*, p. 7, first line.

double-dotted French classical style, harshly scored for brass and piano, the key being F sharp minor, relative of A major, with gritty false relations. Despite its affinity with *Les Biches*, this is music of a severity unprecedented in the earlier work, and something approaching a tragic dimension emerges when, with a shift to 5/4, a 'weeping' cantilena in Aeolian A minor wails over a pizzicato bass (see Example 10). Even when the tempo irons out into common time, Diane meanders irresolutely, as the music reveals her deeper distress. The rocking minor thirds in the bass grimly recall the introductory music.

But the rondo, a dance for Diane's attendants in rapid 2/2 and at first in vernal A major, promises light and grace, for they, unlike Diane, have no need, or at least no desire, to leave adolescence behind. The rhythm (crotchet followed by two quavers) conveys juvenile excitation for the attendants while hinting at anxiety for Diane. When she herself appears—in the major of the upper mediant, C sharp, bristling with seven thorny sharps and with the rhythm diminished to quaver followed by two semiquavers—the effect is that of a distraught polka, with the thirds still ambiguously major–minor. Diane's first appearance thus suggests a dishevelled girl rather than a goddess; and though the next rondo episode sounds less unhinged, with energetic sevenths leaping through a syncopated accompaniment, the 'sortie' of Diane and her 'troupe' has a tinge of hysteria as, never letting up on its ta ta-ta metre, it recapitulates both the C sharp major and the A major tunes. There's a slow fade-out, with flat sevenths and seconds, but without ritardando. The last sounds are minor and major thirds, rumbling on timpani, fatefully if quietly.

In the next dance the attendants prepare Diane's toilet, while

28

the sun rises. The 2/2 tempo is very fast, the theme a brief, blithe fanfare in C major, modulating sharpwards to the dominant. The music is childishly cheery, celebrating the dawning day. Episodes in the relative minor, suave sequential modulations, and a tune 'doucement chanté' over an augmented fifth, slightly perturb the infantile frolic, and enharmonic puns creep into the coda: to which the final cadence, although 'sans ralentir', unexpectedly proves to be in F. Nevertheless, this F major cadence is not fortuitous, for it allows Diane to sweep in in darkly lugubrious F minor. In general her 'Récitatif', serving as an introduction to her dance-aria, is in Heroick French style, with double dots, sweeping scales, and cadential trills; but figurations are spiky and tonality is confused, first moving up the cycle of fifths from F minor to D minor, then plunging even deeper into the abyss than the F minor she started from. The gulf between innocence and experience, in Blake's sense, is manifest as her dance descends from B flat minor to E flat minor, and then into labyrinthine double-flatted areas wherein she is engulfed in 'the blind mazes of this tangled wood', as was Milton's frigid Lady in *Comus*. For both girls the tangled wood is their own sexual fear and fever. In desperation, Diane accepts a ceremonial 'arc' from one of her attendants, who want her to join them in a (pre-puberty?) love-rite. Pressing the bow to her heart, she surmounts the insinuating boogie-rhythm into which heroic French *notes inégales* have been transmuted.

The fateful minor thirds still pad in the bass; and it is from them that Diane, grown up, can effect a clear modulation to E flat major and can, in that heroic key, dance her Dream of Love: an andante with a vocally lyrical theme involving rising fourths and sixths. This melody is Mozartian in both its yearning and its assuagement, which is not surprising since it adapts material from a Mozart divertimento. This dance-aria contains all Diane might have known, and may still know, of love fulfilled; that her dream is not escapist is evident in the middle section, which modulates urgently, with heroic dotted rhythms thrusting down the scale. In the approach to the da capo the motif of 'weeping' semiquavers wails on oboe and flute; these Gluckian instruments, sounding at once 'calme' and 'douloureux', dominate the da capo itself. Solo piano has the love-song as coda, approaching grandeur in an ostinato of fourths and sevenths, and finally of the ubiquitous minor thirds (see Example 11). But it would seem that Diane recognizes that her dream, although truer than truth, is 'only' a dream as she

Example 11 *Aubade*, p. 22, last two lines.

is presently situated. She hurls away her bow of love and, in lunatic despair rather than stoic dejection, bounds into the forest to a triplet gallop in an F minor exotically chromaticized.

Reminiscences of the Toccata figuration recur, though this scene's rebarbative textures are far from being 'emporté'. Indeed, the weeping motif from the first 'Récitatif' and the climactic love-dream reappears in frenzy instead of pathos, for this is music of a Wild Woman of the Woods. Yet abnegating Diane is allowed an apotheosis, since she is not really giving up on life, but rather recognizing that she must leave her infantile bed of roses—a truth already latent in *Les Biches*. The 'Adieu et Départ de Diane' is truly heroic; and although it owes much to neo-classic Stravinsky, metamorphosis into quintessential Poulenc is guaranteed by the fact that Diane's painful agony is also his. Solo piano elides chords of A minor and C major with added seventh, creating static chords of a dominant thirteenth.

Saying goodbye to her friends is bidding farewell to childhood. This is spelt out when Diane now spurns the offer of another bow of love from one—significantly 'la plus jeune'—of her playmates. Massively euphonious homophony gives way to sparse polyphony for woodwind, as Diane 'embrasse ses amies' to a melancholy mutation of the 'weeping' theme of her 'désespoir'. Telescoped chords of A minor and of C major with flat seventh peter into horn and bassoon incantations, transmuted from the first bars of the work, with the D sharps enharmonically altered to E flats. This makes a link with the climactic love-dream in that key; but after a bitonally whirring cadenza for piano and woodwinds, the bassoon incantation is transferred to an 'expressif' cello, meandering through major and minor thirds and through perfect and imperfect (tritonal) fifths. The cello sounds like young Diane with a 'broken' voice! But the conclusion renders the personal universal, as a slow-swaying procession of crotchets leads to an ostinato prophetic of the magnificent end to Stravinsky's *Symphony of Psalms*, first performed in the following year, 1930. Poulenc's ostinato, with subdominant and tonic chords on alternating beats, continues for twenty-three bars, mostly of 4/4, though with occasional truncations to three beats, while orchestral figures float impassively in Aeolian A minor, tinged with Lydian fourths. This prompts a reference back to the severe theme of the Prelude to the Toccata, resounding in middle register on horns. Now, by way of the noble ostinato pattern, the pain of that initial theme is absolved, but not resolved. At least tomorrow is another day; 'brusquement le soleil parait dans tout son éclat. C'est le jour.'

If we accept this as an apotheosis, it can only be in terms of Poulenc's own psychology. As a boy, he had tried to live in the 'paradise of archetypes and repetition' beloved of children and savages. *Aubade*, set at the dawn of a new day, concerns the need to put away childish things, to break out of that endless charmed circle—interestingly identifying its passivity with the female principle. Diane-Poulenc does sunder the bonds, but the act, if triumphant, is also tragic; three years later Poulenc admitted that *Aubade* had been composed 'dans la mélancolie et l'angoisse': qualities audible in the circular ostinato that ends the piece. On a grander scale this evolution from 'preconsciousness' to consciousness was Stravinsky's fundamental theme: hence the technical parallels between the minor and the major master. Poulenc had neither Stravinsky's inexhaustible inventiveness, nor Satie's unshakeable single-mindedness, to encourage him to continue on that lonely path. Even so, we cannot regret that, as manhood succeeded childhood and adolescence during the 1930s, Poulenc became a 'social' composer not in the environment of the Noailles' elegant drawing-room, but in the wider context of the life of France.

Corroboration of this account of *Aubade* is offered by the fact that when the work was publicly performed—in the Théâtre des Champs Elysées, where *Les Biches* had had their Parisian première—the choreography was refashioned by Balanchine, who modified the scenario to incorporate the story of Diana and Actaeon. That the change enraged Poulenc must mean that he resented the intrusion of a male dancer who negated the woman's solitude. That solitude was or had been Francis's own, related to the spiritual chastity he had inherited from Satie. Needing to grow up in his own way, he hated Balanchine's perversion of his integrity. How far this crisis in Poulenc's psychological life bears on his homosexuality would be tricky to estimate, and is perhaps irrelevant to a book primarily about his music. But there can be no doubt that the mythic character of Poulenc's art is related to his personal history, and that this helps to explain the potency of his appeal. In this work his experience of the agony of adolescence stands, *in potentia*, for anyone's, including yours and mine.

3
POULENC, LE DANSE, ET LA BELLE FRANCE

1. Piano Works of the 1930s: Napoli, Les Soirées de Nazelles, Improvisations, Intermezzi, Nocturnes, Suite française, Mélancolie

The music of Poulenc's first phase is remarkable for the candour with which it lives and breathes childhood, this being his legacy from Satie. Francis associated his childhood with Nogent-sur-Marne, where he spent so much time at his grandparents' country house. Even so, Poulenc, unlike Satie, was a social being, who refashioned his art accordingly. During the 1930s and 1940s, his life-style changed, for he divided his time between his Paris apartment and his elegant and spacious country house, Le Grand Coteau, at Noizay in Touraine, where he enjoyed playing the country squire but resisted the attempts of the villagers to elect him mayor. His ideal life was poised between Paris and 'une solitude coupée de visites d'amies', his circle of friends being unusually eclectic. On anti-aircraft duty in 1940 he writes to Pierre Bernac—his partner in song and the closest friend of his life—of his delight in consorting with soldiers and their girls ('Philemon is a former lion-tamer who married his Baucis years ago in Turin, where she charmed snakes'). At the other end of the social scale he writes in 1944 to the Comtesse Jean de Polignac about 'an album of photos of Paris which charms and lulls me like a shot of morphine. . . . What an endless stream of memories come crowding in: the fragrance of the magnolia in the hallway; your perfume in the first corridor; the scent of thyme at the turning to your mother's door; and of greengages and peaches in my own.' Such Proustian retrospection reminds us of Poulenc's passionate affection for painters like Bonnard and Vuillard, especially for their interiors, which reveal the superfices of social life in relation to qualities beyond sociability. There are affinities between these paintings and the social music of Poulenc's middle years, as distinct from his effervescent youth.

A passage from an 1898 letter of Vuillard illuminates Poulenc's transition from the crisis implicit in *Aubade* to his later work.

'There was in my life,' wrote Vuillard,

a moment in which either through personal weakness or through a lack of solidity in my basic principles, everything was demolished. In this wild tempest I had no other guide than my instinct, pleasure, or rather the satisfaction that I found. Happily for me, I had friends. With their help I believed in the simple harmonies of colours and shapes.

Vuillard's delight in acceptance, even of objects that might be considered in 'bad taste', is paralleled by Poulenc's relish for the clichés of social music; for him too it was 'just as easy to understand a vulgar thing as it is to understand a sanctioned thing that has moved you'. He even wondered if this acceptance might not be the essence of modernity; paradoxically, to be 'modern' might be to rediscover the familiar. Proudly, Poulenc admitted that 'I am not the kind of musician who makes harmonic innovations, like Igor, Ravel, or Debussy', while claiming that 'there is a place for NEW music that is content with using other people's chords'. He had confidence that 'the personality of my harmonic style will in time become evident'; and so it did, as Poulenc's Satie- and Stravinsky-inspired muse increasingly embraced French traditions, from the gentle hedonism of Bizet and Gounod (for whose *La Colombe* Francis lovingly provided recitatives), to more substantial relationships with Saint-Saëns, academician, organist, and *petit seigneur*, and with Fauré, a conservatory teacher whose reverence for Bach's linear and spiritual *gravitas* flowered in Parisian salons. Most of all, Poulenc found an *alter ego* in Chabrier, *homme moyen sensuel*, art collector, and vivacious amateur composer whose flirtings with Wagner did nothing to undermine his partiality for *opéra bouffe* and café-concert. Chabrier was a man after Poulenc's own heart: as is evident in the small book Francis wrote in homage to him. Civilized, witty, sensuous, yet exuberantly earthy, Chabrier was the representative upper-middle-class Frenchman from whose example—abetted by that of men like Bizet, Saint-Saëns, and Fauré—Poulenc fashioned an idiom which, if conservative, is *sui generis*; few composers are so immediately recognizable. This middle-years music veers between animal hedonism and humane sensuality; between eupepticism and dolour; between elegance and (in the strict sense) vulgarity. And as with all true hedonists, 'les plaisirs de Poulenc' are shadowed with impermanence. A haunting tune may suffer a disturbing modal alteration; an infectious rhythm may haltingly skip or limpingly add a beat or half-beat; the 'clair' harmonies may be clouded in chromatics or enharmonies, the texture wistfully effaced in Poulenc's favoured 'halo de pédales'.

We have noted such effects in the works of his 'jeunesse', notably *Les Biches*, *Concert champêtre*, and *Aubade*: to which we must add two minor piano pieces that are transitional to the more harmonically and tonally developed (and therefore conservative) style of his middle years. In 1927 Poulenc contributed a *Pastourelle* to a ballet cobbled together by ten composer friends, and privately performed at the salon of Jeanne Dubost under the title of *L'Eventail de Jeanne*. In transcription for solo piano Poulenc's *Pastourelle* became immensely popular: perhaps because it sounds like a reworking in dance terms of the first movement of the seminal *Mouvements perpétuels*. The key is again B flat major, the tempo 'modéré', the time signature 4/4, and the bass defines a primitive ostinato: an oscillation of tonic and dominant crotchets, with a rising and falling scale in the tenor register. The melody, like that of *Mouvement perpétuel 1*, combines gentle repeated notes with stepwise movement, but is now a formalized tune, rather than a linear pattern. The first four-bar phrase stays in the tonic, incorporating a dissonant major seventh into the final triad. The answering clause modulates conventionally to the dominant, but is capped by a metrically irregular incantation over parallel sevenths. Dissonant appoggiaturas are decorated with 'antique' mordents, and the *enfantine*-like tune is recapitulated in more spacious registration, with cadential trills.

A middle section in the tonic minor is strictly a trio, being in three real parts, in the Dorian mode on A flat. A restatement of the invocatory arabesque merges into a da capo of the 'enfantine'; a coda is then appended, abruptly in the tonic minor. Minor thirds thud in the bass, beneath syncopated thirds in middle register. In the penultimate bar the minor thirds change to major; and after a silence there is a loud, 'sec', B flat major chord in first inversion (see Example 12). This coda is oddly disturbing; perhaps it foreshadows the growing-up that, two years later, will be the theme of *Aubade*. Certainly the transitional nature of *Pastourelle* depends on the fact that its shadow on the grass is minatory. What's to come is still unsure, but might be something nasty in the meadow, if not the woodshed. Yet Poulenc preserves a civilized equilibrium in that the final major chord *can* be heard as comical.

Example 12 *Pastourelle*, p. 4, last six bars.

Another work, started as early as 1922 but not finished until
1925, is transitional in a different sense, for the suite *Napoli* is
exotic in subject, conceived on quite a large scale as virtuoso
piano music. Both the scope of the piece and its evocation of for-
eign popular cultures point to paths Poulenc was to explore during the 1930s and 1940s. Especially subtle is the first piece, a
Barcarolle in 12/8 elided with 6/4, with stepwise-flowing cantilena in the right hand and major–minor bitonality in the left,
because what are notated as E sharp appoggiaturas may sound like
F naturals, oscillating to the F sharps of D major. Out of a basically two-part texture Poulenc creates a wondrous wateriness; the
pedal effect at the end is magical. Scarcely less poetic is the *Nocturne*, which also floats a stepwise cantilena over a pedal note,

haloed with a spread chord of the ninth. The modality is Dorian on A flat, disturbed briefly by a fierce triple-rhythmed middle section in remote D major, with false-related thirds.

The third movement, *Caprice italien*, is a brash kaleidoscope of big city life, with the panache of Scarlatti's Neapolitan evocations and a touch of the pianistic sophistication of Albéniz's *Ibéria*. The piece starts with a gallop in a presto 6/16, and in bright E major. Any celestial overtones associated with this key can here only be of the 'see Naples and die' order, for low life, rather than the concert hall, make for a music that is raucous, comic, and slightly scary, as Naples often is. Flamenco-like roulades, emulating guitars and mandolins, lead into a Neapolitan serenade blackly in A flat minor, in a swaying 4/8. But a fast *valse* in the major is embraced within the serenade which, on its return, indulges in military repeated notes, in a rhythm not far from a polonaise. This ethnic plurality is typical of Naples and in a general sense of modern life. Although the coda reinstates E major, there is no da capo of the gallop, only a virtuosic blast of toccata figuration divided between the hands and dispersing in a bitonal puff of smoke. *Napoli*, if not characteristic Poulenc, is most effective pianism. Its exuberant vitality helped him to reinvoke his native France—the sun-baked Morvan as well as Paris—effecting an equation of the parochial with the cosmopolitan. There is a parallel with Dufy's lustrous portrait of a piratical-looking Neapolitan fisherman, iridescent in reds and blues as he proffers an immense fish in a basket. (The picture is now in the Paris Gallery, New York.)

Dufy's comment that he wanted to reconcile irrepressible fancy with ordered lucidity—emulating his revered master Matisse whose 'Luxe, calme, et volupté' of 1904 had been Dufy's most potent inspiration—sounds pertinent to Poulenc also. Francis, we recall, had associated Dufy especially with the music of his Nogent childhood; and we can see what he meant in Dufy's delightful scene of boaters on the Marne (painted in 1925). The vernal colouring, at once sensuous and transparent, the childish cut-out figures, the drifting boats, remind us of Poulenc's 'La Grenouillère' of 1938 (discussed in Chapter 4, Section 2). And one might say that a relationship with Dufy is manifest in much of the social music of Poulenc's 1930s and 1940s. Dufy's desire to 'render beauty accessible to all by putting order into things' was in tune with Poulenc's intentions; painter and composer alike celebrated 'les plaisirs de la vie', usually in conditions of some affluence. Poulenc's piano music of the 1930s repeatedly finds parallels in Dufy's paintings of morning sun on a vase of flowers; of elegant horses cavorting on a race-course, watched by no less elegant human beings; and of *fêtes champétres* of light-irradiated (usually young) men and women. Dufy's famous 'Still Life' of 1928 (now at the Evergreen House Foundation in Baltimore) provides a perfect backcloth for Poulenc's social music: diaphanous light and toyshop houses in the distance, in the foreground a luncheon table bearing bread, wine, fruit, vinegar, with glowingly green folding chairs awaiting imminent guests. Far from being 'nature morte', this still life is vibrant with recollections and anticipations, affecting in charm, surprising in wit. Such qualities distinguish too Poulenc's largest solo piano work, *Les Soirées de Nazelles*, a sequence of variations or 'sketches' which, although sometimes exhibitionistic, is domestic music before being a recital piece.

The virtuosity of *Napoli* reminds us that Poulenc might have been a concert pianist had he wanted to. Even though he hadn't, his natural keyboard skills encouraged him to regard the piano as his basic medium for social music. For fairly polite French society the piano was still a 'home' instrument, and most of Poulenc's piano music is domestically functional. It may not always be easy to play, since it calls for a subtle spontaneity, but it is not, as modern piano music goes, technically formidable, and is happiest when played to oneself or one's friends. Such was the overt intention of *Les Soirées de Nazelles*, for each variation or section was improvised as a portrait of or tribute to a friend or acquaintance, perhaps in conscious emulation of Couperin's portraits for harpsichord. Begun in 1930, the sequence was added to and revised until 1936. For some reason—not, surely, because of the *ad hoc* nature of its origins—Francis was condescending about this chain of adroitly written piano pieces, which makes a possibly profound, certainly touching, psychological survey of 'la condition humaine'.

The 'Préambule' fuses a social *valse* with keyboard virtuosity, and pathos with charm; characteristically, the coda opens windows on perilous seas that may well be forlorn. If most of the 'variations' *are* gracious social music—individual recastings of Chabrier, Saint-Saëns, and the Fauré of the *Valses caprices*—they have human and humane interest. Listening to the sequence of variation 6 ('Le contement de soi') and variation 7 ('Le goût du malheur') one realizes how responsive Poulenc is to contrarieties beneath the social façade. The jolly café tune of no. 6 is as unbuttoned as Chabrier, seeming—as Chabrier claimed to do to his own music—to 'rebondir comme un jeune jaguar'; yet it neither effaces nor is effaced by the sequent variation, a melody 'effleurie' in a hazy web of dissonance. The end of the work is as impressive as its Préambule: for a rather grand cadenza, showy yet intense, explodes into a finale that begins as an Offenbachian cancan, is transmuted back into an amiable *valse*, and ends with wistful gestures of friendship to 'pleasant evenings in the country, with friends grouped around the piano'. The work's final chord is sonorously affirmative—unexpectedly after the gentle, even genteel, 'politesse' of the immediately preceding pages, yet predictably in that friendship was, for Poulenc as for Vuillard and Dufy, an ultimate verity. Domestic music-making, after a good dinner at Nazelles, may embrace a wide range of experience, as well as many sorts and conditions of people, within the charmed and charming circle.

Among the piano works of the 1930s and 1940s Francis awarded pride of place to the *Improvisations* which, although so called, are classically rigorous in form. Their improvisational quality lies in their intimacy, and in the circumstances in which Poulenc hoped they would be performed, for they are not—even the relatively few showy pieces—recital music. Written during Poulenc's vintage piano years between 1932 and 1934, the *Improvisations* are of high quality, mostly in simple ternary or rondo form. We may comment on a few of the pieces. No. 1, in B minor, alternates two contrasted ideas that none the less make unity from duality: a whiplash motif of decorated appoggiaturas around rather than in B minor is juxtaposed with a lyrical tune in 2/4, mostly in four quasi-vocal parts. This turns out to be a middle section, basically in F sharp minor, of a ternary form which modulates to the major, only to be wrenched back to a da capo opening in a 'Neapolitan' C minor, before whisking off into a coda in the original B minor. Typically, the effect, though startling, has classical precedents. Against this the second Improvisation, in A flat major, is as tenderly songful as the first number is metrically fierce. The texture flows in euphonious thirds, slightly ruffled by false relations, which become explicit, and sharply dissonant, in a major–minor cadence in C. The opening clause is repeated and modulates, in richer scoring, to the dominant before returning to the tonic, though there is no straight recapitulation of the

39

child-like tune, and the final cadence is again not in A flat major, but in C major–minor.

Improvisation no. 5 is a chromatic invention based on A minor, and mostly in four real parts, in seductively syncopated rhythm. Sensuality and pathos are married and the coda, resolving over a tonic pedal on a *tierce de Picardie*, melts the heart. Typically, Poulenc follows this with its polar opposite in no. 6, one of his bugle-call marches in the instrument's basic B flat major, and in military metre. Structurally, this is a rondo, and some of the episodes move from parade-ground to bar or circus. The piece ends not in the tonic but in its subdominant, a literal as well as emotional deflation.

The seventh *Improvisation* in C major must be mentioned because it illustrates Poulenc's expansion of range during his middle years, despite the fact that it opens like one of his early 'enfantines', with an undulating white-note tune over a purring semiquaver accompaniment. The middle section of the ternary form is in a C minor that thinks it might be E flat major, and modulates sequentially flatwards. The layout on the keyboard becomes opulent, like middle-period Fauré, and the climax rivals that master in discreet sensuality. After such outgoing passion, the coda restores the vernality of the white-note tune, but clouds the coda with bitonality, affording glimpses 'over the rainbow'. The last C major triad with flat seventh harks back to the final chords of the *Mouvements perpétuels*, as well as to the comparable passages in *Les Biches, Concert champêtre*, and *Aubade*. What is new is the suavity of technique and of feeling, whereby the piece becomes domestic music in the same sense as are Fauré's *Nocturnes, Barcarolles*, and *Valses caprices*.

But perhaps Poulenc's most subtly representative piano work of the 1930s is the modest *Huit Nocturnes* which, although composed over the decade from 1929 to 1938, sound as though they were intended as a totality. These nocturnes are not romantic tone-poems like Chopin's or Fauré's, but are rather night-scenes, sound-images of both public and private events. The first, in C major, has a typically touching tune rotating, in Poulenc's white-note 'enfantine' manner, around the C major third. In the conventional eighth bar it modulates to the conventional dominant, while the left hand weaves a web of conventionally arpeggiated quavers. But a middle section moves beyond the confines of salon or parlour by way of sequentially related concords and ever more fluid modulations. The da capo begins irregularly in A flat major; arriving back at C, it turns into an extended coda, swaying in Stravinskian style between tonics and dominants before disintegrating into a weird epilogue, 'le double plus lent'. Enharmonically related concords process in triple time, to cadence with added seconds glowing around a tonic triad (see Example 13).

Example 13   Nocturne no. 1: coda, last bar of line 3 and whole of last line.

If Poulenc's preludial piece is not necessarily a nocturne, except in so far as it is good to play to oneself of an evening, it makes an appropriate curtain-call to the second number, a nocturnal genre-piece. Entitled 'Bal de jeunes filles', it is unsurprisingly in A major, in common time, and 'très animé'. The *biche*-like young things would seem to be indulging in a quadrille, a dance with both military and theatrical associations. The tune is dotted-rhythmed, with repeated semiquavers between the melody-notes, inducing a slight giddiness, both literally and in the colloquial sense. A modulation to the upper mediant gives the girls a lift, but after returning to the tonic A, the music modulates *down* the cycle of fifths as the tune drops from treble register to cadence on the keyboard's lowest note. There's a double bar, followed by a unisonal modification of the tune in remote F minor. But there is no real middle section, since the quadrille returns fleetingly in F sharp minor, and passes through sundry tonal adventures before its recapitulation in the original A major. Again, the coda changes the perspective. Suddenly 'très lent', the 'bal' cadences through a ripe if slightly painful ninth chord on to an A major triad with added second, only to float off wispily in a *minor* triad. This is a delicious Poulenc image for the vulnerability of youth, perhaps even for the vanity of human wishes (see Example 14).

Example 14   Nocturne no. 2, p. 8, last line.

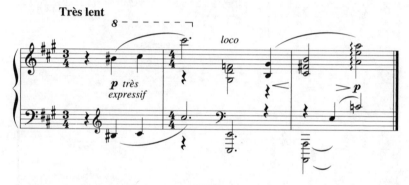

The third *Nocturne*, 'Les Cloches de Malines', is a different kind of genre-piece, for it aurally depicts a small-town market-square that is probably, at dead of night, destitute of people. Bells toll through fourths between F and C, played by the left hand in equal crotchets but irregular metre, as though the mechanism is defective. It may well be, since the bells are very old, being in one of Poulenc's 'antique' pieces—with the proviso that its world, however ancient, is still extant. The tune in the right hand—in the Aeolian mode on A, notwithstanding the F major tintinnabulations—rings 'clair' until dissonances accrue when the texture garners flat sevenths. The tolling bell fades on oscillations between F and C, and is succeeded by a silence that may be ominous, for the cacophony that eventually forms a brief middle section is indeed 'agité', as well as 'mystérieux'. One suspects a programmatic intention; per-haps these frantic clangings warn of some disaster, or maybe the clock's works have gone crazy. In any case, we hear the raucous chaos in psychological as well as physical terms: the hubbub is the ills that flesh is heir to, the slings and arrows of outrageous fortune, things that go bump in the night. After another fraught silence, the bells groan to extinction and the little Aeolian tune, with its now gently tolling F and C, restores the primal scene.

'Bal fantôme', the fourth Nocturne, carries a quotation from Julien Green: 'Pas une note des valses ou des scottisches ne se perdait dans toute la maison, si bien que le malade eut sa part de la fête et put rêver sur son grabat aux bonnes années de sa jeunesse.' So we are left in no doubt that this is an exercise in nostalgia, in which the chromatic harmony, sensuously spaced, lends fragrance to an old-world, dotted-rhythmed waltz. The double dots make the lilt wearier rather than more seductive. Drooping appoggiaturas, cadencing through masking chromatics on to tonic C, sound inevitable, even welcome.

'Phalènes' is a night-scene to balance the town square of Malines. 'Presto misterioso', these moths flicker in iridescent bitonality based on D minor. There is a lyrical 'middle' in the region of B major, leading into a perky tune related to, though not identical with, the first theme. This is a very pictorial piece, the coda to which, quivering over sepulchral minor thirds, is minatory as well as mysterious. Again, one suspects a human allegory: we may be the moths, jitterily directionless.

The sixth Nocturne is again outdoors, wafting through darkness. A stepwise-moving tune in G alternates with a chromatic undulation as tight as the first theme is relaxed. Broken but calm arpeggiated fifths accompany the first theme, and there is a passionate climax to the middle, before the themes are recapitulated in reverse order. The open-fifth arpeggios dissipate into silence and the coda, mutating E major unisons to an E flat major triad in first inversion, resolves gravely and mysteriously on to G *minor*.

The next piece, in E flat major, would seem to reintroduce those *jeunes filles*, now strolling or dancing in a balmy summer night. A guideless tune—a typical Poulenc invention—flows in arches, with an arpeggiated accompaniment luminously spaced. The Fauréan middle is more rhythmically energetic, though no less lyrical. The da capo smiles sweetly but wistfully, especially in the chromaticized cadence. Since the young girls are recalled in this nocturne, it makes sense that Poulenc should round off the cycle with an epilogue, designated as 'Nocturne pour servir de Coda au Cycle'. It starts with a tune close to that of the prelude, but in 3/4 instead of 4/4, and in sharper G major instead of C. This suggests a positive evolution, reinforced by the pulsing quavers that make the tender harmony. The figuration is unbroken as the music modulates flatwards, reaching remote D flat before resolving back to G. But the coda—returning to the unrelated concords of the coda to the preludial piece—ends on bare fifths of C, not G: so the tonic C basic to the suite is reinstated, but not strongly affirmed. Fallibly human, Poulenc mistrusted definitive answers. This delectable suite displays the loving care with which Poulenc defined, and protected, his vulnerabilities, even though they are less patent than those of the *jeunes filles*.

In the cornucopia of Poulenc's piano music the *Suite française* occupies a crucial position. It was written in 1935, originally for choirs of brass and woodwind, with harpsichord acting as catalyst between them. When the composer transcribed the work for piano solo it proved popular; judging from the frequency with which Francis included it in his recitals, it would seem that he himself had a soft spot for it. No doubt he enjoyed the degree to which the suite makes the past present: for the movements are arranged from dances written or transcribed by the sixteenth-century French composer Claude Gervaise, who became a mask for Poulenc, as Pergolesi had been for Stravinsky in his *Pulcinello*. The suite thus sheds light on Poulenc's renovations of 'old' French music, such as we commented on in discussing *Les Biches*, *Concert champêtre*, *Aubade*, and 'Les Cloches de Malines' from the piano *Nocturnes*.

The first dance, 'Bransle de Bourgogne', is an arrangement by Gervaise of what was once a folk-dance. The brisk tune is in Ionian C major, though it opens in an 'enhanced dominant', with sharp sevenths in G. The first clause is harmonized diatonically but with bagpipe-style open ninths; the cadence is unequivocally in C. The second clause is stretched to ten bars, and all eighteen bars are repeated in modified scoring. The bagpipe sonorities are more overt, and the end of the first clause is bitonally harmonized (see Example 15). Effects like this have been referred to as 'wrong note' harmony, though in a sense the wrong notes are right, since they emulate the tangy sonority of Renaissance instrumentation.

The pavane, in a grave 2/2, begins in Ionian F major, the tune launched by repeated notes and with treble and bass in contrary motion. The piano version imitates the brass–woodwind antiphonies of the original, and even offers analogies to the bits for

44

Example 15 *Suite française* (piano version): 'Bransle de Bourgogne', p. 1, last two bars, and p. 2, first two bars.

[Gai, mais sans hâte]

solo harpsichord. The answering clause shifts from F major to Aeolian D minor, introducing passing dissonances that sound 'authentic' but aren't. In a middle section thicker, six-part textures characterize ten irregular bars starting from telescoped A minor and C major triads, offering a glimpse of distant vistas. The final cadence to the 'middle' is a *tierce de Picardie* surprisingly approached by an augmented fifth. The da capo is strict but ends not in F, but in the Aeolian mode on D.

'Petite marche militaire', despite its sixteenth-century source, sounds like Poulenc's bugle-band music, and is jauntily in an F major that sports the bugle's two flats, since it is F Dorianized. The 'pas redoublé' tempo is brusque as well as brisk, each six-bar phrase being repeated. A brief middle section eliding diatonic triads in Stravinskian style is to a degree deflating and perhaps debunking: an effect enhanced when dominants and subdominants clash obstreperously against the B flat major triads, so that the norms of progression in European music sound instantaneously. After a da capo of the original tune Poulenc guillotines the piece with an off-key triad of G major with added major seventh. The effect is not so much farcical as functional—as though the bands-men wanted out, needing a pint.

There is also a technical reason for this startlement, since the lift up a tone introduces the 'Complainte', a haunting eight-bar melody in 6/8, in the Aeolian mode on G. The tune is at first presented monodically, but has a tail that wafts chromatically through pedal Ds, originally played on solo harpsichord; the effect is indeed 'très plaintif'. Chromaticism then pervades the three parts, over a tonic pedal. The music fades on an unresolved seventh chord, with added notes. 'Bransle de Champagne' is another folk-dance to balance the opening number. In the Aeolian mode on G, its effect is hypnotic and, as Poulenc suggests, 'mystérieux'. This contrasts with the 'Sicilienne', which is in C major, with no modal flavouring, though occasional chromatics sound sweetly 'mélancolique'. The coda, built on descending sevenths and simultaneous tonics and dominants, declines grumpily, and slightly comically, until we are left with a single high C, bell-like. Bells take over for the last movement, called 'Carillon'. Entirely in white-note C major, it makes a merry racket until it ends on, not in, the dominant. Bells are oblivious of beginnings, middles, and ends, being almost an acoustical fact of nature. This is relevant to the way in which Poulenc's remakings of old music belong to his and our present.

At the end of his 'piano years' Poulenc composed, in 1940, a substantial piano piece called 'Mélancolie'. If *Suite française* is a climax to his first phase's rediscovery of 'old' France, 'Mélancolie' sets the seal on his affiliations with his immediate predecessors. Perhaps the advent of war conditioned its deep nostalgia and high romanticism: for its melancholy has nothing to do with the Renaissance notion of the melancholic 'temperament', but rather inculcates dreams which, even or especially if they are beautiful, are of their nature illusory. The melody, in sensuous D flat major, aspires from yearningly repeated notes into rising fourths, while the accompanying figures, lying graciously beneath the fingers, are 'très envelopé de pédales'. The dreaminess of the piece lies in its often enharmonic modulations, floating from D flat to C to D majors, and thence to B minor. A figure of repeated notes in the bass carries the music forward, releasing impassioned, triple-rhythmed permutations of the theme, and climaxing in celestial E major: only to dissolve in sequential modulations and chains of trills that might be warbling birds. Middle-period Fauré is the

46

closest musical parallel, but Poulenc, later in date, sounds more unreal, his dreams that much more elusive. We may recall our comparison, early in this chapter, with the luminous domestic paintings of Bonnard, Vuillard, and Dufy. This is epitomized in the magic coda: a melancholy melodic descent, provoking a tonal declension into double-flatted mystery—B double flat against D flat major, a device possibly remembered from Ravel's 'Ondine'. The melancholy is not, however, despair; the final major triads gleam lucently, with only one, very high, 'wrong' note to add edge to euphony.

2. Sextuor *for Piano and Five Wind Instruments (1932–1939); Concerto for Two Pianos and Orchestra (1932)*

While the piano was Poulenc's most direct route towards his socially orientated music of the 1930s, there are larger works that contributed to that end. A keywork is the Sextet for piano and wind instruments, which, like *Les Soirées de Nazelles*, is transitional in the obvious sense that it was some years in the making, started in 1932 and finished only in 1939. The first movement is an outward-going romp more rococo than baroque in style. The upward-sweeping scales in the introduction pay homage to French heroic idiom, while also having something in common with the scales in the first movement of Beethoven's Third Piano Concerto. When 'le petit train-train de la vie' gets going it is undermined by continual shifts of key, perhaps with echoes of Prokofiev's Third Concerto. As with the Trio for oboe, bassoon, and piano, we expect a rococo rondo-sonata, with subsidiary themes in remote keys; but no sonata movement accrues. The hurly-burly of everyday life once more unrolls on a collage principle, until a tipsily honking horn puts the brake on. Solo bassoon, lyrical but metrically irregular, heralds the 'middle', at exactly half tempo of the first section, of what proves to be an expansive ternary structure. The luscious tunes are introduced by the piano, then taken up by wind soloists, entwining in quasi-operatic dialogue, with written-out turns. Rococo Mozart and Rossini merge into the Gounod or Massenet said to nestle in the heart of every Frenchman, for both the contour of the themes and the ripe harmonic sequences belong to ninetenth-century French romanticism. The da capo of the allegro is much curtailed, and is rounded off by a coda in which the horn is syncopatedly inebriated. The end

47

is brusquely in youthful A major, the more refreshing after the time-travelling through French and European history.

The slow movement, which is not very slow, inverts the structure of the first movement in that, while being again in ternary form, its middle section is twice as quick, instead of twice as slow, as the first and third sections. Its key, D flat major, is an upper mediant to A; level chords on piano support song-like tunes for the wind instruments, with leaping fifths and sixths and quasi-operatic turns. Rococo pastiche evokes a dream world, as in the Trio for oboe, bassoon, and piano; yet the dream is mocked when the middle section, elevated from D flat to E flat, becomes a fast gallop in oompah rhythm. The horn, nightmarishly bounding through octaves, teeters between pathos and farce. The da capo of the first section, invigorated by the jaunty middle, is in A flat major, dominant of the original D flat; but a brief coda, in unisonal dialogue between piano and wind, transports us to a very dark A flat minor.

The finale enhances the rumbustiousness of the first movement. Boldly marked 'prestissimo', it is a collage-type rondo that pluralistically admits to 'other kinds of experience' in its episodes. Solo horn is goatish in caprice, always 'sans ralentir' at that. The main theme is an Offenbachian gallop in 2/2; and there is usually a disparity between this eupeptic frolic and the episode tunes that aspire upwards, savouring their operatic cantilena with no slackening in pace. The end, after a rather grand episode in C major, is as unexpected as it is unfrivolous. For the music stops on a dominant of C; tempo becomes 'très lent'; and solo bassoon initiates a coda wherein wind instruments chant permutations of the song-themes, 'très doux', in a compromise between C major and minor, with gently padding chords from the piano. The work sways to rest in a stillness as solemn as the ostinato end of *Aubade*; that shadow on the grass is hardly less daunting, in this piece that would seem to be unabashed entertainment, than it had been in the major achievements of Poulenc's twenties.

In the year in which he started the Sextet, 1932, Poulenc also composed a Concerto for two pianos and orchestra: a work intended for the concert-hall, though it is sociably entertaining and was originally played by the composer and his friend, Jacques Février. In a letter to Paul Collaer Poulenc refers to the work's 'bigness, energy, and violence' which, he believed, accounted for the impact it made on audiences. Although a bravura piece, it was central to Poulenc's development, a successor to the crucial *Concert champêtre* and *Aubade*. Despite and because of its high spirits, the concerto 'grows up'.

It opens with irresistible brio. After two brusque D minor chords, the first piano chatters in parallel fourths while the second piano oscillates, xylophone-like, between semiquaver As and B flats. The rapid, patterned ostinatos recall the 'paradise of archetypes and repetition' beloved by Poulenc in adolescence, though in this case increased momentum generates recognizable 'themes'. Scales spurting in both directions induce a shift from basic D minor to remote C sharp minor: in which key the soloists bounce a 'très sec' arpeggiated theme, which intermittently jets skyward, to cascade in chromatic scales. A second tune, beginning in F major (relative of D minor) is bandied around without establishing identity as a second subject, though its 'enfantine' character contrasts with the fiery brilliance of the main material and generates, instead of a development, a middle section at around half speed. This begins over an ostinato of a G major chord with added minor second and flat seventh, the cantabile tune being based on repeated notes in dotted rhythm. The pianos garland the tune with whirling scales, though the toccata-figuration does not return in its pristine shape.

Instead, there is an abrupt climax and a long silence, followed by a curious coda, suddenly slow and 'très calme'. The orchestra murmurs in quaver triads derived from the bassoon 'organum'; first piano weaves ostinato figures in the Phrygian mode on D; second piano returns to the oscillations between high As and B flats, as heard in the first bars of the concerto. Now, being 'lent' and 'très egal' as well as 'mystérieux et clair tout à la fois', the effect is not so much that of xylophones as of a celestial gamelan, though the more direct source is probably Satie's acrobats and jugglers (see Example 16). The glassy texture, in the context of the music's previous energy, is not synonymous with the 'green paradise of childish loves' that Poulenc had cultivated in his youthful pieces about growing up, especially *Les Biches* and *Aubade*; but it casts a spell, and the movement, still unruffled, flickers out in a pianissimo dissonance and a 'très sec' cadence to a quiet D minor triad.

The larghetto, although at first sweet and gentle, doesn't thus discount our 'Western' world. Its theme, in B flat major over an Alberti accompaniment, is overtly Mozartian, but changes when

Example 16 Concerto for two pianos: first movement, p. 18, last line.

[Très calme]

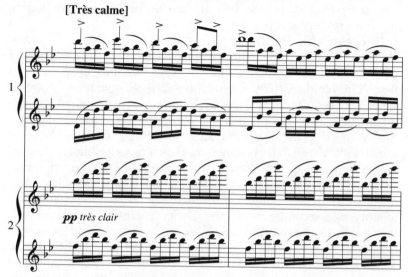

the first piano modulates in chromatics to the subdominant, and leads into a middle section, 'beaucoup plus allant', with a dotted-rhythmed theme in A flat. Here we are closer to Saint-Saëns than to Mozart; and the dotted rhythm stays consistent as modulations range in modest agitation, until we reach a cadenza over a dominant pedal in B flat. As so often with Poulenc (and with his friend Milhaud), the da capo is much curtailed. The final bars telescope tonics and dominants of B flat; only here does the sonority relate this 'European' movement to the quasi-Balinese coda to the first movement.

But the finale suggests that West and East may have achieved some *rapprochement*. It opens as a whirlwind toccata with a D major key signature, though tonality is chromaticized and textures are sparse. The first theme is a very fast gigue in quaver triplets in 2/2; the second theme drops the key signature to become a dotted-rhythmed march, initially in B flat minor. The sizzling triplets generate a third tune, flowing spaciously in A major, and freely modulating to find its way back to the quasi-military tune, now rather grand in B flat major. There is no orthodox development and little recapitulation. Tunes and figurations meld blithely in collage, in sociably Saint-Saëns-like charm and Chabrier-like effervescence. Suddenly, the chattering breaks off; after a 5/2 silent bar, the 'gamelan' itself, now loud and clattery, no longer induces a childish trance but rather encourages us to accept the brusque procession of ninth chords that introduces the ultimate, unambiguously minor triad of D. Poulenc's sun often casts shadows; here he welcomes them and finds, in his synthesis of East and West, another metaphor for growing up. In our barbarous century occident and orient needed one another if they were to survive. In his modest way Poulenc here reinforces truths explored by greater men—such as Picasso, Stravinsky, and Messiaen.

4
POULENC, LA VOIX, ET L'AMOUR

1. Poulenc, Max Jacob, and Le Bal masqué

Despite his partiality for the dance—so exuberantly manifest in the two-piano concerto—Poulenc was convinced that 'essentially I am a man of song in all its forms'. Whereas he had shaky confidence in his ability to handle large instrumental forms he was, in the basic song-form of the 'mélodie' with piano accompaniment, 'afraid of no-one', proud that there was something he could do better than most. Few would now doubt that some of the songs he wrote in the 1930s and 1940s are, however restricted their genre, great music. For these songs Poulenc did not abandon the poets who had moved him in early youth, though he added others, notably Paul Eluard, who 'always brought out the best in me'. But the first song-cycle of the 1930s, *Cinq poèmes de Max Jacob* (1931), set a poet whom Francis had known well in youth, but had not previously musicked. We may bracket the cycle with a secular cantata to words by the same poet, written in the following year; both are an apotheosis of le Danse and la Belle France, and both are works for which Poulenc nursed a deep affection.

Max Jacob was a Jewish poet, novelist, and painter who, born in 1876, had moved to Paris in 1901, where he became a crony of Picasso and Apollinaire, and through them of the adolescent Poulenc. Francis recognized in Jacob another Janus who shilly-shallied between God and the Devil, describing him as 'a great-hearted and sensitive man, a Venus of Bohemianism, who ended his life in exemplary devotion!' The verses Poulenc chose for his cycle concerned Jacob's Breton childhood, being character-sketches spoken or sung by juveniles or adolescents. He wrote the songs at Nogent, 'où j'étais venu passé deux mois en 1931 dans ma maison d'enfance, toute vide mais pleine de souvenirs. Je ne peut jouer cette mélodie'—the last number in the cycle—'sans penser à mon chien Mickey, couché sous le piano.'

In the first number a Breton girl, still a child, babbles of her lost pet chicken and little cat; asks sundry peasants if they can help her find them; but ends by imagining a mass concert of countryside birds, 'playing trumpets for the King's banquet', though she doesn't reveal whether this is in triumph at her pets' return, or to inure her to, or comfort her for, their loss. The music harks back to the child-like paradise of *Mouvements perpétuels*, beginning with a piano ostinato teetering between chords of C minor and D minor, while the voice pipes a runic incantation. The avian concert is Satie-like, vocally wavering between F sharp and G, while the piano's right hand warbles aloft in tweeting grace-notes and the left hand, 'doux et poétique', decorates a ninth chord over a pedal C. Musically, there is no evidence that she recovers her pets. She consoles herself in a brief trance until the 'sweetly poetic' chord, fading out, is dismissed by a gruffly percussive C on the piano.

The girl of the second song, 'Cimetière', would seem to be in her early teens, for she has a sailor-boy, and will end up in the cemetery if, as seems likely, she is deprived of him. The tune is a small ballad rather than a nursery rune; the key is warm A flat major and the 6/8 rhythm, beginning on an up beat, is tenderly yearning. The lyricism recalls the simple art-songs of Bizet or Gounod rather than folk-song, though there are folk-like melismata in the refrains about an emblematic rose and lily. The last stanza envisages the sailor's return; but she seems to admit, as the lovely tune droops in chromatics and in cross-rhythms of two against three, that she is dreaming of 'notre enfance, quand nous jouions sur le quai'. False relations between A flat major and F minor give piquancy to the piano part; a low percussive bump, changing the final A flat major chord to F minor, is again dismissive.

In his 'diary' of his songs Poulenc says that 'Cimetière' has 'the atmosphere of the artificial wreaths of pearls that can still be bought at the grocer's. It's all a little like a garish colour print.' Typically, he advises the performer to sing it 'quite straightforwardly'; and this is still more apposite to 'La Petite Servante', in which he admits to being 'directly inspired' by Moussorgsky. There is a natural affinity between the Russian bard of child, peasant, and simpleton and Poulenc in his 'enfantine' manner, for there his sophistication is only skin-deep. This song is a charm, praying for the saints' protection from thunder and lightning, and from the devil as their agent or cause. The middle section, built over a comically sinister revolving cam, is a catalogue of plagues, ranging from pimples to leprosy, with which the Devil will afflict us if we don't watch out. That this is another childish spell is clear in the last stanza, when the girl prays that she may grow up quickly, and find a good husband. The music sways 'avec charme' in more than one sense, at first in the Aeolian mode on F but shifting to A flat major, with tinges of its relative, F minor. Ambiguity is pointed, for the girl, with the realism of child and peasant, doesn't expect much from marriage: only a husband who isn't too much of a drunkard, and doesn't beat her *every* evening. The final reverberation of a D minor triad, with little relation to the rest of the song, is another stroke of psychological acumen.

Indeed one might say that the difference between the songs of Poulenc's first 'enfantine' phase and the Jacob songs of the early 1930s lies in the fact that whereas the *Bestiaire* songs follow Satie in entering into a child's mind and world, the Jacob songs, in admitting psychological awareness, relate the child to the adult. This is evident in 'Berceuse', sung by an adolescent baby-sitter who is rocking a squawking infant in a cot, while father is out at mass and mother at the cabaret—an inversion of roles appealing alike to Jacob and Poulenc. The girl reflects on the baby's possible demise of croup, colic, or diarrhoea, which would leave her free to go shrimping at low tide. The music begins as a fast *valse*, modulating as the girl grows desperate. By the last stanza tonality has shifted from the initial G major to very sharp regions, only to sink back, as the shrimping expedition seems illusory, to G.

The final song, 'Souric et Mouric', begins as a regression to early childhood in being a nonsense ditty about a mouse and a rat. But it covers the transition from preconsciousness to consciousness in that the rat and mouse teach a spider lurking in a kitchen cupboard how to spin a 'beautiful linen cloth', which can become a commercial commodity in Paris, thereby earning enough to buy an orchard, a meadow, three cows, and a bull for stud. The last stanza, however, relinquishes commercial enterprise in being a nocturnal about life on the newly acquired farm, where one may learn to sing by harking to the blackbirds, magpies, and tree-frogs—an agreeably eclectic orchestra. Musically, the song begins as a spiky scherzo, turns into a gallop for the trip to Paris, but is transmuted into Satiean lyricism and pattern-making for the nocturne, the melody drooping scalewise in pastoral F major. It is still a child singing ('très blanc'), but he or she is on the verge of whatever mysteries night may hold.

This Jacob song-cycle was a trailer for the 'cantata profana' *Le Bal masqué*, written in the following year to a collection of farcical verses that gave Francis the feeling of discovering 'an old photograph in a holiday album'. He loved the music he made for these verses from *Le Laboratoire central* because it was redolent of his Nogent self, and because it was still close to, if more extrovert than, the music of his godfather Erik Satie—especially in the fairground manner of his ballet *Mercure* (1924). Poulenc devised this theatrical entertainment for the Comte and Comtesse de Noailles, who three years previously had commissioned his *Aubade*. The jolly *Bal masqué* complemented that somewhat desperate work, indicating that he had come through adolescent crisis enough to be able to laugh at it. Having survived, he felt no need to apologize for his one-time juvenility, and could have, for *Le Bal masqué* 'toutes les indulgences. Je suis certain qu'on n'aime pas véritablement ma musique si on le méconnait. C'est du Poulenc cent pour cent.' He added that between them *Le Bal masqué* and *Quatre Motets pour un temps de pénitence*—the gravely intense choral work he was to write in 1938—gave 'une idée très exacte de Poulenc-Janus', and that each side of the coin weighs equal in the balance.

Le Bal masqué is scored for baritone solo and an ensemble of oboe, clarinet, bassoon, trumpet, piano, violin, cello, and percussion—sonorities exploited with the pungency of Satie's fairground musics. The tootling tunes, the patterned figurations, the march and dance rhythms, are presented without suspicion of parody. Poulenc warns the singer that he should '*croire* avant tout aux mots qu'il débite. Pas de réticences, pas de faux airs entendus, pas de clins d'œil complices.' This is precisely the advice he had offered to the singer of his first, most Satiean mini-masterpiece, *Le Bestiare*; and it is worth noting that the surrealism of Jacob's verses, as transmuted in Poulenc's music, is often associated with specific memories from the composer's childhood. Thus in the 'Préambule' Madame la Dauphine is projected, in a brisk 2/2 on nasal oboe and tangy cornet, with the precision of an infant's dream or nightmare. Similarly, in the third and fifth movements Malvina and La Dame Aveugle are fabulous beings momentarily identified with flashbacks to childhood. Malvina 'se tirebouchonne une valse tzigane . . . le petit doigt en l'air'; while the blind woman of Jacob's poem finds herself identified with

a stout lady of independent means who, around 1912, frequented the Ile de Beauté at Nogent-sur-Marne. She lived in a chalet, half Swiss, half

55

Norman, and passed her life playing patience, sitting on her front doorstep attired in a dress of black silk. On a cane armchair a few steps from her sat a man who looked like Landru, with pince-nez and a cyclist's cap, reading his newspaper.

Poulenc was 13 at the time, and it must have been the acuity of his memories—in turn released by Jacob's 'subconscious' images—that gave such vitality to the music. 'L'atmosphère banlieusarde qui m'est chère' was evoked 'grâce aux mots de Max, pleins de ricochets imprevues! . . . C'est l'atmosphère des crimes en chrome du *Petit Parisien* des dimanches de mon enfance. "Quelle horreur", s'écriait à cette epoque le cuisinière de la grandmère. Encore un type qui a assassiné sa belle-soeur! Il se pourrait que LA DAME AVEUGLE ait subi le même sort!'

Although the potency of this work is musically inseparable from the Satiean economy of its scoring, Poulenc moves bodily into the street, making a music more vulgarly extrovert than Satie's. Especially in the instrumental interludes, such as the Bagatelle, Poulenc's 'musique foraine' has mud on its feet, sweat on its brow. The final 'Caprice' is café music with no holds barred: except for a brief passage when the 'frénétique' gallop is chilled by a sinister, fourth-founded tango. Poulenc did not exaggerate when he claimed that 'au bout des vingt minutes que dure *Le Bal masqué* le public doit être stupefait et diverti comme les gents qui descendent d'un manège de la Foire du Trône'.

2. Poulenc, Apollinaire, Paul Eluard, Louis Aragon, and Louise de Vilmorin: Banalités, Tel jour, telle nuit, Fiançailles pour rire, Montparnasse, Cé

If the Max Jacob song-cycle and cantata belong with Poulenc's 'Nogent' music of childhood and adolescence they also betray, as noted, the beginning of a process of 'psychological' awareness. In particular, the Jacob song-cycle leads on to the music of his middle years, in which French poetry, the human voice, and the theatre dominate. It is to the point that in 1931, immediately after the Jacob songs, Poulenc returned to his first collaborator, Guillaume Apollinaire, setting a sequence of four poems in his more psychologically penetrative style. In 1938–9 he capped these Apollinaire settings with others—notably a single song 'La Grenouillère', and a cycle with the deceptive title of *Banalités*.

'La Grenouillère' (the froggery), despite its date, is perfect

56

Nogent music, setting a poem which Francis had toyed with over many years. As he put it in his journal:

'La Grenouillère' évoque un beau passé perdu, des dimanches faciles et heureux. J'ai pensé à ses déjeuners de canotiers, peints par Renoir, où les corsages des femmes et les maillons des hommes ont d'autres accords que de couleurs. Evoque aussi, avec mon égoisme habituel, les bords de Marne chers à mon enfance. C'est l'entrechoc de leurs canots qui rhythme d'un boût à l'autre cette mélodie tendrement lancinante.

The rhythm of the oars in the piano part's wide-spaced, D major-rooted chords accompanies a stepwise-moving melody that is indeed 'très las et mélancolique'. Both tune and pedal-haloed piano drift with the tide, though the flatwards subsistence towards the end doesn't rock the boat. Flattened appoggiaturas enrich the cadence, but the final major triad, rippling the water, fades to silence.

In his *Journal de mes mélodies* Poulenc recounts how, having returned to Noizay in October 1940, he was browsing in his library and, lighting on his long-beloved Apollinaire, found tears welling to his eyes as he reread the 'délicieux vers de mirleton groupés sous le titre de *Banalités*'. He chose two poems from the collection to add to two others he had been meaning to set for years, and added, as prelude, a separate poem inserted in a prose work of the poet. This last number, 'Orkenise', Poulenc had originally thought of as a marching song; but in the *Banalités* cycle he treats it 'rondement, dans le style d'un chanson populaire', and in triple time. Orkenise is a road in Autun leading to the Roman gate: which may be why the tune slightly swaggers over a repeated pedal note on F. The vocal melody is in Dorian F minor; the piano part is tinged with major–minor bitonality. On the road a tramp, leaving his heart behind as he departs from the town, passes a carter entering the town with his heart aflutter because he has come to be married. Volatile modulations mirror these complementary destinies, but the walking pulse stays constant. The pedal Fs, with their bitonal embellishments, return in the coda; people come and go, hearts still ticking, whether in hope or despair.

The second number, 'Hôtel', leaves the open road for a Montparnasse hotel where the poet, having no desire but idly to smoke, basks in the sun that 'passe son bras par la fenêtre'. Musically, the song resembles 'La Grenouillère' in that ripely chromatic, slow-swaying chords in D major accompany an arching melody, the phrases of which droop in languid appoggiaturas, but finally rise in semitonic content (see Example 17). It is revealing that in this café-concert number Poulenc's musical 'images' are so nearly identified with those which, in 'La Grenouillère', express nostalgia for his childhood haunts at Nogent; the innocent and the experienced Poulenc are the same man.

Example 17   'Hôtel' (from *Banalités*), p. 5, last line.

Cannily, Poulenc places next to this enervated indoors song his setting of a strange poem, 'Fagnes de Wallonie', that evokes the wild outdoors. The love-sick poet is tramping over the Walloon uplands, hoping to calm his distress by listening to the birds and beasts in the fir plantations, and in sniffing the fragrance of the heather, though the wind is implacable. The folky melody flows stepwise in the Aeolian mode on F sharp, though there's a patch of limpid A major for the sweet-smelling heather. The tree-torturing winds at the end provoke false relations without sundering the 'seul élan', and the final cadence, 'toujours sans ralentir', is in F sharp major. Perhaps Francis had a peculiar fondness for this poem—which he had been intending to set for years—because in it the turbulance of adolescence is momentarily appeased.

'Voyage à Paris', like 'Hôtel', is an instance of Apollinaire's inspired doggerel, set as a fast French *valse* in E flat major. It is slightly more than a bon-bon, because the lilting tune convinces us that Paris, as compared with any 'pays morose', was created by and for love. But its point in the cycle is to provide relaxation before the long final song, which sets one of Apollinaire's finest poems to music worthy of it. If 'Fagnes de Wallonie' concerns the pangs of adolescent love and 'Voyage à Paris' is a shrug of the shoulders dismissing its turmoil, 'Sanglots' confronts the pain at the heart of love, which we are ourselves responsible for, though it seems also to be 'reglé par les calmes étoiles'. All lovers are dreamers whose love, even if their hearts must break, are all they know of truth: 'laissons tout aux mortes | Et cachons nos sanglots'. Poulenc's musical image opens calmly, with the piano melody swaying between fourth and fifth over pedal notes on tonic F sharp and dominant C sharp: a pendulum that reflects the 'eternity' of the stars. The vocal melody havers between Dorian and Aeolian F sharp until the swaying fifths shift to E flat minor, when the stepwise-moving melody is richly harmonized in broken chords. But the pulse remains *un*broken as pace accelerates, reaching climax at the reference to 'malades maudits de ceux qui fuient leur ombre'. At this point there's an enharmonic twist from E flat minor to E minor: which is really a Neapolitan F flat that immediately returns to E flat minor and the swinging pendulum, at the original tempo. Again, interior tensions accrue, but are resolved in a heart-warming, if also heart-breaking, phrase built on a leaping sixth, sequentially harmonized (see Example 18). Eventually, the original modal F sharp minor is re-established, though not the original themes. Leaping octaves and sevenths sound consummatory after those aspiring sixths, but they tell us that 'rien ne sera libre jusqu'à la fin du temps'. The 'sanglots' are audible, even

Example 18 'Sanglots' (from *Banalités*), p. 18, ll. 3 and 4.

palpable, in the approach to the final cadence which, after an anguished appoggiatura on a G sharp minor triad, fades through crystalline chords to the most irremediably minor triad. That this great song could provide an epilogue to a cycle called *Banalités* is typical of Poulenc; the common round is not always common.

Apollinaire, Jacob, and perhaps Cocteau were the poets of Poulenc's boyhood; having grown to man's estate, he found inspiration in the poetry of Paul Eluard, whom he had first met in the same crucial year, 1917, as he had encountered Apollinaire and Satie. 'I immediately took to Eluard', Francis said, 'because he was the only surrealist who tolerated music, and because his entire output is sheer musical vibration. . . . If my tomb could be inscribed: Here lies Francis Poulenc, the musician of Apollinaire and Eluard, I would consider that my greatest claim to fame.' Yet Poulenc did not set Eluard in those early days, and his tribute to him may explain why: although Eluard's surreal aspects linked him to Apollinaire and to Poulenc's youth, the poetry of his mature years used surrealism to different ends. If still a way back to the spontaneity of a child, surrealism was now also a key to darker depths in the human psyche, the more so because Eluard's maturity coincided with the Second World War and with the abasement of France during the German Occupation. Whereas Apollinaire died young, Eluard, born in 1895, lived to become the major poet of France during those years. Poulenc grew up with him; felt strong enough to set him in 1935; and in 1936–7 composed to Eluard's words his song-cycle, *Tel jour, telle nuit.* 'Eluard', Poulenc remarked, 'was my true brother—through him I learned to express the most secret part of myself, and especially my vocal lyricism.' Nor can it be fortuitous that, in the year in which Poulenc first set Eluard's poetry (1935), he entered into his collaboration with Pierre Bernac, forming a voice and piano duo that survived for twenty-years and was, in artistic distinction, rivalled only by the duo of Benjamin Britten and Peter Pears. Despite Francis's homosexual proclivities, he and Bernac were not lovers; but the mutual understanding and the moral and artistic inspiration they afforded one another can hardly be overestimated. *Tel jour, telle nuit* was written for Bernac, and contains the finest among the ninety-odd songs Francis was to write for his friend.

The Apollinaire cycle, *Banalités*, makes a whole, despite the disparities in mood and length of its constituents. *Tel jour, telle nuit* contains nine rather than five songs, and the poems are all short. Even so, the whole they add up to has a certain grandeur that comes from the intensity with which they surreally explore the 'interiority' of love. As the title indicates, the cycle concerns basic dichotomies: day and night, light and darkness, good and evil, life and death. Although the verses are love poems, their subjective intensities embrace the destiny of a nation, as well as that of the lovers. Their images probe within and open outwards: which is why Poulenc's musical images, complementary to those of the poetry, became a storehouse on which he drew for the rest of his life.

The first song, 'Bonne journée', is typical in that its positive qualities contain their own negations. On this lovely day women seem lovely and loving; men look carefree, and shadows skitter away like mice in a gutter; clouds massed under dark trees suddenly vanish, 'drenching' the heart with dawn. Yet the light contains the darkness, as the darkness promises the light. This is mirrored in Poulenc's music. The vocal melody, marked 'calme', floats up through a C major triad intensified with a tritonal F sharp, accompanied by a (still Satie-like) ostinato of rocking octaves. This may be a pendulum of envious and calumniating Time such as will recur throughout Poulenc's music, with sundry, sometimes contradictory, implications. In this song, each stanza starts from the same point but modulates flatwards, the basic tonality inclining more to C minor than to C major. Only in the dew-drenched last stanza does the highest note, A flat, resolve on to the fifth of C. The piano's pendulum now vibrates between open fifths, the rhythm of the initial octaves being preserved by the low, syncopated Cs. There is no third, major or minor, but a flat seventh, creeping into middle register, carries us outside Time (see Example 19). We have frequently noted this effect in Poulenc's early music; the difference is that this song, though greenly paradisal, touches depths as well as heights.

In the second song, 'Une ruine coquille vide', depths are uncovered; for the poem offers an image of desolation—children playing in the shell of a ruined house. The scene is surreal in that it juxtaposes game-playing children, in whom life goes on as best it may, with a decay of human artefacts; although the song predates the war, we cannot but respond to its private desolation with reference to later, all too public, events. Poulenc's music, 'très calme et irréal', complements this by floating a stepwise-moving vocal line over bells swinging in 3/4 on the piano, pene-

Example 19 'Bonne journée' (from *Tel jour, telle nuit*), p. 3, last line.

℗. *(sans changer jusqu'à la fin)*

laissez doucement vibrer; strictement en mesure

trating softly syncopated chords of G minor with flat sevenths. The bell-ostinato survives through chromatic and enharmonic modulations, with an effect between dream and nightmare. But the latter takes over in the next number, 'Le Front comme un drapeau perdu', a 'lost' song in which both the poet and his love are like to drown. Poulenc's setting, though 'très animé in tempo, begins serenely in the Aeolian mode, becomes momentarily pentatonic when the lovers' hands meet in the water, but returns to Aeolian A as the stone sinks. In the last bars the left hand's leaping octaves recall the time-measuring pendulum of the first song; but the *tierce de Picardie* makes submersion in the waters a baptism.

There is no hint of redemption in the next two songs, which are brief but terrifying. 'Une roulette couverte en tuiles' finds an objective correlative for inner anguish in a scene 'out there'. A gypsy stands by her caravan and a dead horse, while her child beats his fists against a pitiless world. So vividly is the image objectified that Poulenc says in his *Journal* that he himself saw, or imagined he saw, the gypsy woman's enraged child 'late one November afternoon in Ménilmontant'. He sets the poem in recitative 'très lent et sinistre', to a procession of crotchet chords meandering between major seconds, major thirds, and diminished fourths, virtually without tonality, though anchored by pedal Ds. The last words link the external scene to ourselves: 'Ce mélodrame nous arrache | La raison du cœur.' It ends vocally 'dans un souffle' and pianistically on an unresolved dissonance, 'très sec'. All this happens in one slow page of score; and the next song is even shorter, since although the score covers two pages, its tempo is prestissimo. If the previous song is externalized, 'A toutes brides' is internalized, for its whirlwind describes a ghost-lover who is invited to surrender 'au feu qui te désespère'. It gravitates towards a ferocious G minor in a *moto perpetuo* of semi-quavers, always 'sans ralentir'.

Neither of these two brief songs would make much sense outside the cycle; one of the ways in which *Tel jour, telle nuit* is a keywork lies in its interlocking of fragments to create a totality in a waste land. Poulenc explicitly says that 'A toutes brides' serves mainly as a prelude to 'Un herbe pauvre', a small miracle musically equivalent to Eluard's marvellous poem. The poem 'simply' describes a blade of grass new-born in a frozen landscape; Poulenc's music, 'clair, doux et lent', *enacts* this in the rudimentary device of a modulation from E minor to its major, and by a transparent da capo of the original frail tune in the original key, 'sans ralentir' (see Example 20). This makes the new life and the deathly snow co-existent, as they are. Poulenc said that for him this poem had 'un goût divin'; but the moment, though magical, is fleeting, for the next two numbers enact the tempest that the 'herbe pauvre' had withstood. 'Je n'ai envie que de t'aimer' throbs in 12/8 quavers, in dark B flat minor, shattering human love in sweeping the beloved into a cosmic oneness with nature: a theme intensified in 'Figure de force brûlante et farouche', in which negative forces take over. Poulenc tells us that he was deeply moved in writing this song, in demonic D minor and initially at a savage presto. Breaking off in abrupt ferocity, the song turns into a 'morne' incantation at the point when 'La vie se refuse', the voice trailing around a nodal B flat while the piano's left hand drifts in major thirds between A and F. When 'le sang au dessus d'eux triomphe pour lui seul' the piano whirs between the notes of a diminished seventh, and in a coda the rocking octaves of the first

64

Example 20 'Une herbe pauvre' (from *Tel jour, telle nuit*), p. 13, ll. 1 and 2.

song return, now with menace. But the end—on the words 'cette santé bâtit une prison'—attains heroic resolution in D major, with the voice on high A.

The final song, 'Nous avons fait la nuit', is epilogic, dealing directly with the identity of opposites. A rising scale motif, similar to that of the first song and likewise accompanied by padding quavers, is now in the Aeolian mode on C. Although it is a love-song, the woman is both lover and stranger, and the admission of *not* belonging is essential to the love fulfilled. Poulenc remarks of this song that 'il est bien difficile de faire comprendre aux interprètes que le calme dans un poème d'amour seul donner de l'intensité. Tout le reste est baisers de nourrice'. This his music demonstrates when the C minor aria is metamorphosed into unsullied C major, consummated in a piano postlude the more poignant because throughout the cycle the keyboard has seldom operated independently of the voice. This epilogue is as intrinsic to the cycle as are Schumann's piano postludes to his. At the end the floating fifths of the first song are recapitulated, without the major third, but still garlanded with a blue flat seventh, and in this case with a blue tenth (E flat, not E natural) above it.

Tel jour, telle nuit was at once recognized as a masterpiece, and its electrical charge has not weakened during the many performances it has received. Perhaps it is worth noting that the first song is dedicated to Picasso, shortly to be the dedicatee of the Eluard cantata *Figure humaine*, possibly Poulenc's greatest work; that the song about the children in the ruined house is dedicated to Freddy, mother of Poulenc's daughter; and that 'Figure de force' is dedicated to Bernac, Francis's artistic collaborator and moral support. Other fine Eluard settings—notably 'Tu vois le feu du soir'—date from these years, but we must turn to the other 'new' poet whom Poulenc explored during the decade. That he should number a woman among his empathetic poets bears on the ambivalence of imagination and gender that conditioned his art, to climax, in 1958, in his one-woman, one-act opera on Cocteau's *La Voix humaine*. Poulenc's tribute to Louise de Vilmorin is worth quoting in his beautiful French:

Peu d'êtres m'émeuvent autant que Louise de Vilmorin: parcequ'elle est belle, parcequ'elle boîte, parcequ'elle écrit un français d'une pureté innée, parcequ'elle son nom évoque des fleurs et des legumes, parcequ'elle aime d'amour ses frères et fraternellement ses amants. Son beau visage faisait penser au XVII siècle, comme le bruit de son nom. Je l'imagine amie de 'Madame' ou peinte par Philippe de Champaigne, en abbesse, un chapelet dans ses longues mains. Louise échappe toujours à l'enfantillage en dépit de sa maison de compagne où l'on joue autour de pelouses. L'amour, le désir, le plaisir, la maladie, l'exil, la gêne, sont à la source de son authenticité.

Significantly, Poulenc told Henri Hell that Louise re-animated his youth: 'J'ai trouvé dans la poésie de Louise de Vilmorin une sorte d'impertinence sensible, de libertinage, de gourmandise qui se prolongeait dans la mélodie ce que j'avais exprimé, très jeune, dans *Les Biches*, avec Marie Laurencin.'

The most considerable of Poulenc's Vilmorin settings is the cycle *Fiançailles pour rire*, dating from 1939 and, according to the composer, inseparable from the war: 'Sans la guerre je n'eusse sans doute jamais écrit ce cycle. . . . J'ai composé *Fiançailles pour rire* pour penser mieux à Louise de Vilmorin, enfermée dans son château d'Hongrie en 1940 pour Dieu sait combien de temps. Voilà tout le rapport de mon œuvre avec cette horrible tornado.' The subtle femininity of the poems provided the antidote Poulenc needed to that 'horrible tornado', for the apparently slight verses tingle with foreboding. The first poem, 'La Dame d'André', appears to be about a light flirtation between André and a woman met at a country ball, she being unknown to him yet redolent of forgotten ghosts. Will he remember her 'pour son couleur, pour son bon humeur de Dimanche', when winter withers 'la grande avenue aux feuilles blanches | De son album des temps meilleurs'? In an inimical world Proustian retrospection may serve as a bulwark against fear, even as excuse for a smile—as it did for Proust himself. Poulenc's music 'auralizes' this in a flowing A major texture for the piano, and in a no less innocent vocal melody in the Aeolian mode. Fleeting chromatics counteract the innocence, as do the modulations when the first eight-bar clause shifts from A minor to C major and E minor. Tonally, the song flitters through the garden as insouciantly as the lovers, though rhythm and figuration remain unruffled and the tempo directive— 'modéré sans lenteur'—recalls the decorum of Poulenc's no less radically French predecessor, Couperin le Grand. The song's ending maintains equilibrium between hope and regret; the added notes, trembling through the final *tierce de Picardie*, catch to perfection the evanescence of love and life, tingeing lucent A major with dissonances that illuminate, rather than obscure (see Example 21).

In natural sequence, 'Dans l'herbe' is a moving little poem about love and death as mutually dependent; the woman cries to the man who 'est mort seul dans les bois | Sous son arbre d'enfance'. That such a poem would appeal to Francis is evident; it may not be fortuitous that he dedicates the number to the mother of his daughter. The triple rhythm is 'très calme et très égal'; the tonality hovers around, but does not affirm, A major, as it wanders through simple diatonic concords in wonder-inducing relationships. The music moves flatwards to reach a *distant* climax on the realization that 'j'étais loin de lui', but never winds its way back to that 'irréal' A major. The final cadence opts, wide-eyed, for C sharp major, a third higher.

67

Example 21 'La Dame d'André' (from *Fiançailles pour rire*), p. 4, last seven bars.

Poulenc admitted that the next number, 'Il vole', is one of his most difficult songs, not so much because it whirls 'presto implacable' through a piano part 'dans le style d'une étude', as that the poem, and therefore the music, is precariously balanced between the 'concrete' reality of the woman's environment ('le fromage rond de la fable au bec de mes ciseaux de vermeil') and the hysteria latent in the relationship between the lovers. The piano figuration fidgets in chromatics; the vocal line, beginning and ending in E flat, intermittently quivers in terror of her 'amant voleur', and expires 'dans un souffle'. This prepares us for the next song, wherein the woman presents herself as 'un cadavre, doux comme un gant'. The poem again turns on the thingness of things—her eyes are two pebbles—and the vacuity imposed by loss of love. Poulenc's setting is 'très calme' but also 'intense et lié', again proving that only calmness gives authenticity to a love-song ('Tout le reste est baisers de nourrice'). Quaver chords, 'très égal', support the soaring vocal line, in Phrygian E minor. Textures are enriched as tonality is freed, and she seems to accept loss, as children efface painful memories. The piano postlude, settling into a slow-swinging 3/4, resolves into 'celestial' E major.

'Violon' seems to be a simpler poem, describing a scene in a Parisian café, in which a woman hears in the fiddling of the café gypsy the sighs of her own and her lover's hearts. Poulenc tells us that he had a particular Hungarian restaurant in the Champs Elysées in mind. Louise's husband had imported a band from Budapest to entertain its patrons, and Poulenc's music begins as a pastiche Hungarian waltz, in A minor but with momentary shifts to remote keys. The exotic fiddler is emulated in the piano's wailing sixths, double-dotted rhythms, and spurting fioriture: all clichés of the idiom, though, as Poulenc points out, such Hungarian pastiche becomes as typically Parisian as the American rag in Ravel's *L'Enfant et les sortilèges*. The pastiche is precariously balanced between parody and pathos: as becomes explicit at the end, when return to a ripe A major *tierce de Picardie* is dispatched by the gypsy fiddler's dismissive A minor pizzicato.

Trivial, even cynical, reality leaves the woman with her dreams; in the final song these become 'fleurs promises, fleurs tenues dans les bras . . . fleurs des amours fanés'. This is a dream-song which must sound, according to the composer, as though it comes from a remote distance, even from another world. The exquisite melody is in 'très calme' triple time, accompanied by rich but pianissimo chords on each beat, in the sweetness of D flat major, upper mediant to the A major that pervades the cycle. Poulenc does not disturb the serenity when he affects a tiny climax for the 'images saintes'; and when he repeats the opening lines of the poem to a modified version of the original melody, the accompanying chords, though still richer, are higher and even more remote. But the vocal line slowly descends and the final cadence brings us to earth, being minor rather than major. Though this dour minor triad may be an ultimate reality, dreams seem truer than truth.

Fiançailles pour rire are the most representative of Poulenc's Vilmorin settings, though there are other songs of exceptional beauty, notably 'C'est ainsi que tu es' from *Métamorphoses*, which has a nobly arching tune in 'tragic' B minor, with poignantly decorated appoggiaturas. The date of this cycle is 1943, which takes Poulenc into the years of war. Two famous songs are explicitly associated with this war, the earlier being another Apollinaire setting, 'Montparnasse', started in 1941 but not completed until 1945. That the process of composition was so protracted may be because the poem, written in 1912, is so rich in memories ('les oases suscitées par le mot "Seine" ou par le mot "Paris"'), nostalgia being intensified, for Poulenc, by the grim fact of war, and especially by the German Occupation. For Francis, the poem contained the essence not only of Apollinaire, but also of 'Picasso, Braque, and Modigliani'; no wonder the song moved him, as it can us, to tears. The first two lines, which he found very difficult to set, were the last to be completed, in Paris, in 1944. Other lines were set at various times between 1941 and 1943, and the final revision was made in February 1945, the year the war ended. That Poulenc could thus 'assemble' a song over a period of time bears on the kind of composer he was: not so much a 'maker' in Beethoven's sense, as a 'gatherer' of what might have been ephemera of daily life; interestingly, the various 'bits' always recur in the same key.

Apollinaire's poem, though written before the First World War, has applications to the Second: for the poet is gazing at a small hotel in Montparnasse, in front of which stand two 'plantes vertes', now void of flowers or fruit. There are overtones in the fact that Montparnasse is Mount Parnassus, and that the 'bearded angel' who is distributing leaflets outside the hotel is really 'un poète lyrique d'Allemagne'. He wants to love Paris but, being teutonically 'un peu bête et trop blond', is not an effectual lover; his

Example 22 *Montparnasse*, p. 2, l. 3.

eyes are balloons that float off into thin air. Poulenc's setting imbues this metaphor with grandeur as well as mystery. The melody, consistently 'très calme' in 2/4, is in dark E flat minor, with his favourite accompaniment of gently syncopated quavers. Tonality loosens for the young German poet, and the melody expands into falling fifths and aspiring tritones, reaching climax on a high F sharp in E minor (see Example 22). The young German's reveries about Sundays in Paris grow both more seductive and more melancholy as the music wafts through many keys before it drifts, like the balloons of the poem, into 'l'air pur'. Though the piano part returns to E flat minor as the balloons, like our dreams, disappear, it dissolves chromatically, moves through unrelated concords in triple instead of duple time, and cadences in E flat *major*, albeit very softly.

The other famous war song sets a poem of Louis Aragon who, born in 1897, became a leader of the surrealists as well as a committed communist. Poulenc, not being a political creature, set only two of Aragon's poems, one of them being this tragic apotheosis of wartime France, 'Cé'. The poet, having traversed 'les ponts de Cé', has a ballad-like vision of French chivalric history, 'le long lai des gloires fausses'. How false becomes evident in the spectacle of the Loire as it currently is, littered with 'voitures versées et les armes désamorchées': a sight that prompts him to lament 'O ma France, O ma délaissée, j'ai traversé les ponts de Cé'. Poulenc's directive is again 'très calme', and tonality is even flatter than that of 'Montparnasse', for the song is in deathly A flat minor; nor does Poulenc alleviate those seven flats throughout the song, nor modulate during the first nine bars. The piano opens with a monody alternating a tonic arpeggio with stepwise movement. When the voice enters, its melody grows from the piano monody, while the piano accompanies in parallel sixths and then in levelly pulsing chords. As the vision of the presumptively chivalric past unfolds the music slowly modulates, initially to F minor as the 'éternelle fiancée' dances into the meadow, reminding the poet of that long tale of 'gloires fausses'. The music for the eternal beloved is 'infiniment doux' in declining sequences, but may also be unreal in being 'effleurie de pédales', as tonality subsides flatwards. The passage is repeated, with dire double-flattenings, when the vision of the past is replaced by the Loire-as-it-is, though the final cry of 'ma France délaissée' aspires to, but fades on, a high A flat. The piano postlude, cadencing in the major, pays tribute to France in mollifying, though not cancelling, the song's dolour. Characteristically, Janus-Poulenc coupled this noble elegy with his other Aragon setting, 'Fêtes galantes', a patter-song marked 'incroyablement vite, dans le style des chansons-scies de café-concert'; just as he had coupled 'Montparnasse' with a raggily parodistic setting of Apollinaire's 'Hyde Park', marked 'follement vite et furtif'.

Two other cycles of the 1940s call for brief mention, the *Trois chansons de Lorca* because they are his only settings of this great European. In his *Journal* Poulenc expresses regret that he found it difficult musically to express his admiration for Lorca, the violin sonata dedicated to the poet's memory being 'très mediocre

Poulenc', while these three songs 'sont de peu poids dans mon œuvre vocale'. This verdict seems hard on the songs, especially in reference to 'L'Enfant muet', a portrait of a dumb beggar child. Poulenc's piano part begins in unison octaves, wheezing like a hurdy-gurdy in a chant riddled with devilish tritones. The moderate tempo is scrupulously adhered to throughout the wandering chromatics of the F sharp minor melody, for the whining beggar-boy is denatured by his misery. 'Adelina à la promenade' is a quasi-Spanish dance in 6/8 crossed with 2/4. The girl capers by a sea that surrealistically 'n'a pas d'oranges', in a Seville that 'n'a pas d'amour'. The E flat minor song is 'follement vite, dans un tourbillon', and if a scherzo, is more desperate than funny. The third song, 'Chanson de l'oranger sec', also concerns physical and spiritual aridity, being an appeal from the tree to a woodman, asking to be hacked down as penance for its orangeless unfecundity. Poulenc complains that this sarabande is 'nobly' French instead of 'gravely' Spanish. His truly noble melody begins in the Dorian mode on G, with the piano pretending to be a Louis XIV harpsichord. Tonal adventures in flat regions colour the middle section without exacerbating the processional movement. The final stanza characteristically compromises between modal C minor and its major, with blue flat sevenths.

These songs date from 1947. The other cycle, *Chansons villageoises*, goes back to 1943, and differs from the settings of distinguished poetry so far discussed in that its verses, in popular style by Maurice Fombeure, are literally 'village songs' that evoke 'le Morvan, où j'ai passé de si merveilleux étés'. The cycle was originally scored for baritone and a small orchestra used in the style of a small-town French band; Poulenc acutely described the music as 'a kind of *Pribaoutki* from the Morvan'. The gamin-like vivacity of the quick numbers—such as the 'très gai et très vite' 'Chanson du clair tamis' and a 'prestissimo possible' 'Chanson de la fille frivole'—is irresistible; while 'Le Mendiant' has a dourly dramatic intensity, and 'Le Retour du Sergent' is an exercise in Poulenc's childishly bugle-blowing militarism. The one slowish song, 'C'est le joli printemps', is a gem and quintessential Poulenc. The verses are a folky tribute to spring in time of courtship, which must have stirred memories of *Les Biches*. The tune, in dulcet D flat major and flowing triple time, is as simple as a real folk-song, while the sonority glows like early sunshine. The words are a traditional exhortation to gather rosebuds while one may: 'C'est le joli

printemps, | C'est le temps d'une aiguille, | C'est le joli print-
emps | Ne dure pas longtemps'. Only those who are acutely alive
in nerves and senses can create, from the mere recognition of
impermanence, music that tugs at the heart-strings, as Poulenc's
does here.

5
POULENC, LA GUERRE, ET LA MORT

1. Rocamadour: Litanies à la Vierge Noire *(1936)*, Sécheresses
(1937), Quatre Motets pour un temps de pénitence *(1938–1939)*
We have seen that Poulenc, partly through his association with
Eluard, became during the late 1930s and early 1940s a composer
of more serious consequence than had been suspected. This deep-
ening and broadening of range coincided with the advent of the
Second World War; but with Poulenc, as with most genuine
artists, the public dimension of experience was complemented by
a private dimension. If the war was a crisis for France and
Europe, Poulenc at the same time suffered a private psychological
trauma which carried him to the brink of nervous breakdown.
Although this situation was to recur in later life, usually in a sexual context, his first and most momentous crisis in the 1930s
could broadly be called religious.

A Roman Catholic by family tradition, Francis 'lapsed' during
and after the First World War. Yet we have noted how, beneath
the ostensible frivolities of his youth, his heart remained, like that
of his master Satie, of a singular purity: so we need not be sur-
prised that the death of an intimate friend and musical colleague,
in a car crash in 1936, should have shattered him. That the manner of Pierre-Octave Ferroud's death was horrendous—he suffered
what Francis called a 'décollation atroce'—must have given a raw
edge to the experience of loss. Poulenc decided to make a penitential pilgrimage to the shrine of the Vierge Noire at Rocamadour,
where he had a mystical experience, as a consequence of which he
composed, on his return home in August 1936, *Trois Litanies à la
Vierge Noire de Rocamadour.* Although black virgins were icons
quite widely assimilated by the Roman Church, they seem to have
derived from pre-Christian cults of an Earth Mother: for which
reason, perhaps, they were regarded as peculiarly therapeutic,
associated with healing, birth, and even rebirth. The name Rocamadour, whatever its etymology, hints at rock, hardness, bitterness, *and* love. Perhaps Francis, in his dark night of the soul over
Ferroud's death, felt that a black goddess might sympathize with

his agony; certainly he, who had blossomed as an *enfant terrible* in the aftermath of the first war, discovered a religious dimension to his art as the storm-clouds gathered before the war of 1939–45. And there may have been a technical miracle to balance the mystical one, in that Poulenc fashioned, from the premises of French Renaissance polyphony and more commonly homophony, an idiom that is modern in being modally ambiguous and tonally precarious, while preserving the sense of wonder and purity of heart typical alike of the old French chanson and motet and of Poulenc's earliest master Erik Satie, maker of 'messes des pauvres'.

The *Litanies* were not Poulenc's first choral work, for as early as 1922 he had written a very secular *Chanson à boire* as an exercise for his counterpoint teacher, Charles Koechlin. This hardly pretended to be more than pastiche, and was anomalous in that its sixteenth-century model was functionally social—music for drinking to—whereas Poulenc's was a recital piece. That he none the less regarded the male-voiced chanson as of some importance in his canon must have been due to the fact that it unwittingly explored the idiom that was to be the basis of his religious music. The kinship is clear, even though the *Litanies*, scored for a three-part choir of children's or women's voices with organ, are as ethereal as the *Chanson à boire* is jollily gross. A quality one might call visionary is manifest in the sparseness of the organ prelude, 'calme' in its compromise between quasi-medieval organum and acutely dissonant polyphony in contrary motion. The voices, which should be 'whitely' child-like even if they are not of children, plead for the help of God the Father in a stepwise-moving monotone in the Dorian mode, the organ's role being exiguous, 'très doux et aérien'. When the words ask for God's pity on our frailty, stray chromatics flutter the austere modality: which becomes Phrygian on D, shifting, after a brief but harsh organ interlude, to Aeolian on G.

The vocal declamation still moves by step, 'humble et fervent' over a soft organ bass rocking through a G minor triad. Modality is freer as the voices float in parallel $^6_3$ chords, in early Renaissance style, and climax in linear transformations of seventh chords, rising to fortissimo Gs on the words 'Priez pour nous'. The organ reinforces this appeal with a comparably hectoring, chromatic pedal part; and the textures—as the children and we as children address the Black Virgin herself—are gently undermined by false

76

relations. When the text more intimately particularizes, the tempo speeds up. Adressing 'la Reine, à qui Roland consacra son epée', the voices grow declamatory, wavering between D, E flat, and E natural, stimulated by trills and a few fierce dissonances on the organ. For the final section, however, the music returns to its original 'calme' to unfold a radiant cantilena on Aeolian F, with dubieties between the flat and the sharp seventh. The organ laces a single line (on viol da gamba and cor de nuit stops) into the vocal part, whose text—'Dame, dont le pélerinage est enrichi de faveurs spéciales, Notre Dame, que l'impiété et la haine ont voulu souvent détruire'—would seem to bear directly on Francis's anguish over his friend's death.

Pain is healed in the final section, in which the organ's arpeggiated G minor triads are a gentle but durable Rock. The voices discover pathos within repeated tones and the simplest scale figures, over levelly flowing quavers and an ostinato of broken triads on flute stops of the organ. The mode veers between Aeolian and Dorian on G but introduces, with piteous effect, cadential F sharps on the final apostrophe to Jesus. The repeated octave Gs recapitulate the dramatic outburst on the words 'Priez pour nous', with the dynamics now 'très doux et clair' (see Example 23).

In the year following the *Litanies*, 1937, Poulenc unsurprisingly composed his first strictly liturgical work, a Mass for a cappella voices. Written at Autun, in Poulenc's beloved Morvan, it was undoubtedly therapeutic; listening to its luminous part-writing one may sniff the thyme in the air, relish the caress of the sun on one's cheek, and be grateful for a physical and metaphysical grace comparable with that of French Renaissance chansonniers such as Claudin de Sermisy and Guillaume de Costelay, whose music is as fragrant as their names. Poulenc has here resuscitated a singing and dancing tradition that was obsolete, and has done so with touchingly original vulnerability. Modal alterations—especially in the often monodic Agnus Dei—invoke the startlements as well as the holy *mysterium* inherent in the ceremony of the Eucharist, in a manner no doubt conditioned by the outward savagery and inner agony of Ferroud's death. Even so, some more radical musical disturbance was called for if the psychological watershed occasioned by that dire event were to be fully realized artistically. This occured in the *Quatre Motets pour un temps de Pénitence*. which Francis recognized as a turning-point.

Immediately previously, in the summer of 1937 when he'd writ-

Example 23   *Litanies à la Vierge Noire*, p. 15, last two lines.

ten the Mass, Poulenc composed a 'secular cantata' that directly
confronted the 'negative emotions' that a sacred liturgical work
could bypass. In a sense this was fortuitous, since the cantata
Sécheresses was a commission from Edward James, a wealthy English dilettante who had flirted with surrealism and, knowing of
Francis's recent association with Eluard, decided that Poulenc
would be the composer to set James's verses to music. Francis
accepted the commission because the poems' Dali- and Tinguy-
like images of skeletons, pulverized deserts, and waste lands
chimed with his mood in the wake of Ferroud's death, as well as
with Europe's pre-war malaise. He produced a score of unwonted
ferocity, in its aggressive pattern-making and harsh, Stravinskian
scoring, though such angularities are alleviated by passages of
modal polyphony and homophony anticipatory of the crucial
choral work to words by Eluard, *Figure humaine*.

At its first performance the public found *Sécheresses* bewilder-
ing, more because it was not what was expected of its genial composer than because of its intractabilities. That the piece never
established itself in the repertory may, however, be Poulenc's
fault, for its acerbities are not Poulenc 'cent pour cent', and the
strain shows in a sectionalism that doesn't quite come off. Francis
admitted to having made errors of 'auditory vision' inexcusable
from a composer of his age and experience, hinting that he may
have denied his own nature in a desire to please Edward James,
who deserved something he liked in return for his money!

Sécheresses, a highly sophisticated choral work and, for Poulenc,
'advanced' in orchestral terms, is at an opposite pole to the *Litanies à la Vierge Noire*. Even so, Poulenc needed to write it if he
were to discover in his music an intensity adequate to the terror

of Ferroud's death and the miracle of his experience at Roca-madour. In consequence the *Motets de pénitence* are powerfully subjective, even 'expressionist', pieces while being also devotional music that may function as an act of worship in church. The Latin texts are traditional, taken from the liturgy for Holy Week. Poulenc's techniques are also orthodox in musical terms, for the vocal lines start from the rhythms of the words, and grow from, if they do not always adhere to, vocal modality. Thus the first motet, 'Timor et tremor', admits to human frailty but affirms that God 'will not let me be confounded', as the adaptation to the English Prayer Book puts it. In Poulenc's setting each vocal line conforms to Renaissance precedent. At first, all four parts are unambiguously in the Aeolian mode on A, moving note for note. The answering phrase ('Et caligo cecidit') divides the altos *à 2* softly to enrich the harmony, and the phrase ends on the domi-nant of the dominant. But when the voices enter in Renaissance style 'points', crying 'miserere nobis', the mode is again Aeolian, with E as root, returning to A. The painful dissonances at the cadence on the dominant modify Renaissance practice, being false relations between sharp sixth in the ascent and flat sixth in the descent. At the words 'Quoniam te confidet' Poulenc changes the mode to Lydian A major; an occasional tritone creeps into the vocal contours, and modern tonality, to a degree ousting antique modality, equates confidence in God with an affirmation of *human* strengths, as the harmonies, hinting at C sharp minor and F sharp minor, become more functional, with dissonant passing notes and even a 'horrendous' diminished seventh. The word 'confundar' seems to provoke ambiguity, the music moving through unrelated diatonic concords but ending on a radiant chord of A major (see Example 24). Through compromise between old modality and new tonality Poulenc becomes simultaneously a man of God and a modern seeker.

The second motet, 'Vinea mea electa', deals with Christ's justifiable pique about his fate, compared with that of barbarous Barabbas; he finds it difficult to understand why 'all thy sweetness is turned into gall', though he must have known that his Father worked in a mysterious way. Again, the idiom is basically homo-phonic, the rhythms those of the spoken word. Even so, the open-ing is startling: luminous, as though we are suddenly in the divine presence, for the choir is in six parts and the tonality glows in C sharp major, as high up the cycle of fifths as possible. The open-

Example 24 *Motets de pénitence*: 'Timor et tremor', p. 4, last line.

ing invocation—in 6/4 time, 'lento teneramente' and, despite the radiant sonority, 'con malinconia'—gives way to imitative points as Christ asks why sweetness has soured, the sharpness of C sharp major being muted to the four sharps of Aeolian C sharp minor. Passing dissonances enact the 'bitterness', and the contrapuntal points grow more aggressive as fanfare-like triads build a 'tower in thy defence'. The motet ends with a da capo of the C sharp major invocation, now 'dolce possibile', though the C sharp minor quasi-canons stray into very *sharp* dissonances on the word 'crucifigeres'. The end is tonally ambiguous, mirroring God's moral ambiguity: for modal C sharp minor merges into its relative E major, only to conclude with a sustained C sharp major chord, in false relation with the previous E major.

'Tenebrae factae sunt' sets the great passage from the Lenten liturgy, dividing altos and basses to produce six real parts. The tempo is 'très lent', irregularly barred. Although the behaviour of the vocal lines does not deny Renaissance principles, the 'tenebros-ity' of the sonority is exceptional, with first altos and basses grind-ing in semitonic undulation against the second altos and basses, who sustain a tonic B. The first section expands this device, moving from unison to fifth to third, thereby involving a progressive degree of 'humanization' from medieval spirituality to Renaissance physical-ity: which becomes overt at the fluctuating harmonies on the 'ninth hour' and at Christ's frenzied chromatics and dotted rhythms in his appeal, 'voce magna', to his Father. Roots in B minor are not sun-dered by a declining sequence of tritones; and Christ, bowing his head in serpentine chromatics, expires in a *ppp* cadence that sounds like a dominant seventh of C resolving on to a B minor triad. In fact, the F natural of the dominant seventh is notated as E sharp, being an appoggiatura which unfurls on to F sharp: another meta-morphosis of old into new (see Example 25).

'Tristis est anima mea' is the only one of the four motets to call, dualistically, on contrasted sections, and for this reason makes a powerful consummation. It opens, 'très lent', in a variously modal G minor, treble solo dialoguing with the other voices in verbal rhythms, stabilized by frequent minor thirds. The clause declines on to a major triad of the dominant; but the word 'fugam' suggests traditional associations between flight and fugue, and briefly whirling fragments of fugato culminate in boldly repeated crotchets. These pun on the enharmonic identity between E flat and D sharp, thereby cadencing, in dramatic triple forte, on a dominant triad of E minor. Back at the 'très calme' tempo, the voices wail in drooping thirds, and at the words 'filius hominis tradetur', chant in the Aeolian mode on E. Modulating back to G minor, the chant is sundered by an aborted eruption of the 'vos fugam' fugato: this time only a puff of smoke that van-

Example 25   *Motets de pénitence*: 'Tenebrae factae sunt', p. 7, last line.

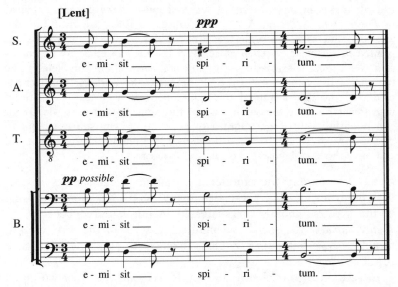

ishes as the chorus sings, with solo treble on top, a consolatory coda. Throughout, basses are rooted on tonic G, rocking between octaves. Above, the voices shift homophonically between E flat major first inversion and tonic G minor in root position. The music enacts the 'immolation' of Christ's sacrifice in a hieratic calm that recalls the liturgical music of Stravinsky, though Poulenc's music belongs to French, not Russian, tradition, and has a human commitment that Stravinsky's lacks.

2. Poulenc, Eluard, and the French Resistance: Figure humaine (1943–1944)

Although the *Motets de pénitence* were unique in Poulenc's work up to that point, it was not long before he produced another choral work to equal them in intensity. This was not strictly speaking a religious piece, though being triggered by the experience of war it involved awareness of love and death, hope and despair. The genesis of *Figure humaine* was recounted in an interview with Claude Rostand:

During the Occupation a few privileged beings, of whom I was one, would receive with the morning mail wonderful typed poems bearing pseudonyms that disguised but did not conceal the authorship of Paul Eluard. It was in this way that I received most of the poems contained in *Poésie et la vérité 42*. After a pilgrimage to Rocamadour, I had the idea of composing a clandestine work which could be prepared and printed in secret and then performed in the long-awaited day of liberation. With great enthusiasm I began *Figure humaine* and completed it by the end of the summer [of 1943]. I composed the work for unaccompanied choir because I wanted this act of faith to be performed without instrumental aid, by the sole means of the human voice. . . . My friend and publisher Paul Rouart agreed to print the cantata sub rosa, and in this way we were able to send the music to London where, before the end of the war, in January 1945, it was broadcast.

It was not merely the emotionally fraught circumstances of this first performance that persuaded many people that here was one of the greatest choral works created in our battered century. In *Figure humaine* the social and political anguish of the war came to terms with a faith that Poulenc likened to 'that of a country priest'.

In relation to the Eluard song-cycle *Tel jour, telle nuit* we noted that although the nine poems are all short, Poulenc's settings produce in sequence an effect of some grandeur. *Figure humaine* also consists of short poems, with the difference that they were intended to form a sequence, and are capped by an epilogic poem of some length. Poulenc, with his experience as a writer of song-cycles, finds no problem in making the cantata's short sections cumulative, and sustains momentum through the long consummatory poem, being resourceful in dealing with the refrain, 'J'écris ton nom'. The name proves to be 'liberté'; and that this complex poem became a clarion-call of the French Resistance demonstrates how a difficult poet may, moved by an urgent, universal theme, become a force in the popular imagination. Poulenc's love of his country, and dismay over its then-desperate plight, ensured that he would devote himself to his task with fervour but without portentousness. The grandeur of the project is implicit in the fact that he dedicated it 'à Pablo Picasso, dont j'admire l'Œuvre et la Vie'; and more practically in his scoring it for two choirs of six (divisible) parts. Poulenc uses his large vocal resources antiphonally, and as a means of achieving a quasi-orchestral variety of sonorities. His skill is both sophisticated and impressive: the more so because idiomatically he holds to the traditional French precedents that had been the basis of all his choral music.

84

Poulenc opens with a poem that opposes a dark night of the soul and of France to the hope (not promise) of a spring that might banish 'monstres' and rehabilitate 'les bons visages sûrs d'eux-mêmes'. It's a heroic extension of the little poem about the snow-rigid blade of grass in *Tel jour, telle nuit*; and Poulenc's massive scoring and 'très large' tempo are apposite to the social and national context. Initially the key is 'tragic' B minor, and the choirs are divided antiphonally; the theme, chanted fortissimo by the basses of the second chorus, is a rising and falling triad with two (quasi-pentatonic) added notes. An acrid dissonance on the word 'laid' shatters this nobility; and the second choir introduces the snow- and death-defeating blade of grass in a modulation to dark E flat minor and then (where else?) to 'infernal' F minor. The defeat of the 'monstres' by the 'bons visages' reinstates an unwontedly euphonious B minor, leading to a belated mating of the two choirs. These cadence by way of an embellished dominant seventh of C on to a B minor triad—the same progression that had ended the penitential motet, 'Tenebrae factae sunt'. Against this gravity, the second number opens as a scherzo, setting a poem about young girls leaping, on a 'grand matin joyeux', from death, corruption, and degradation. Poulenc underlines the verbal theme by direct recollections of Renaissance dance-song, with some of the voices la-la-ing in danced refrains, while others spit out the text in explosive rhythms. Climax arrives in unisons between the choirs, at the passage about 'l'eau vaste essentielle'. A coda is twice as slow, in modally inflected E minor over a tonic pedal. The final triad is blissful E major, with basses on low E and sopranos on high G sharp. There is a psychological allegory in the fact that human 'faiblesse' proves a road to triumph; the pianissimo E major chord here is a prophecy of the very loud and massive E major chord at the work's ultimate end.

The third poem, 'Aussi bas que le silence', concerns death in the heart and shame in the mind, and Poulenc sets it—lurching down a semitone from the previous number—in black E flat minor, in note for note homophony for the second choir. This creates a sense of oppression, even of suffocation; but the final words of the poem—'Crache sa nuit sur les hommes'—change the perspective. For 'les hommes' cadence in E flat *major*, the triad being echoed high, but very softly, by the first choir (see Example 26). Only human beings themselves may confront darkness with hope: so this is linked to the next poem about the seed nurtured

Example 26 *Figure humaine*, p. 24.

patiently in the earth, where it prepares 'à la vengeance un lit d'où je naîtra'. Though the music is still 'calme', the key is now spring's vernal A major, the theme prancing in sixths and sevenths, around an internal dominant pedal. Rhythmic and tonal momentum climax on a dissonance on the word 'vengeance'; but a da capo of the opening ends in a lucent A major triad with sharp sixth and blue flat seventh. Enharmonies suggest the magic and mystery of a new birth.

That this movement is scored for first choir only enhances the excitement of the double-choir antiphony in the next poem, 'Riant du ciel et des planètes'. The poem is both angry and appalled; and Poulenc's setting—in grave C sharp minor, relative of and complement to heavenly E major—is 'très vite et violent', exacerbated by ding-dong antiphony between the choirs. They come together only twice, and then venomously, when we are told that 'les sages sont ridicules'. At the triple forte conclusion the texture is divided into fourteen parts: a 'planetary' fury that introduces the lovely sixth poem, 'Le jour m'étonne', wherein the paw-marks of an animal in the snow presage 'les empreintes de la vie'. This section is sung by the second choir only, with sopranos bearing the burden of the words in a melody floating in the Aeolian mode. From modal simplicity the lines grow tortuous as they seek 'a track of life' through death itself. But the whole-tone enharmonies of the coda-cadence end on a triad of A minor, not major.

Divided choirs are again in action for the penultimate poem, the longest thus far. It tells how death is the god of love, and 'les vainqueurs dans un baiser s'évanouissent sur leurs victimes'. Children are no longer afraid; stupidity, madness, and baseness give way to brotherly men who no longer strive against one another and against life. This may be wish-fulfilment validated by the agony of war, but Poulenc's 'très emporté et rude' setting convinces in calling for the first time on polyphonic, even contrapuntal, resource. The theme, yelled by the altos of the first choir, is highly chromatic, being an eleven-note row in which no tone is repeated (see Example 27). This is a long way from French Renaissance idiom, and departs still further from it as the irregular entries, at any pitch, appear in 'très violent' antiphony. Given the nature of the theme, there can be no defined tonality, though on the crucial phrase 'La pourriture avait du cœur' there is a hint of resolution around F sharp and C sharp. Ultimately, the two choirs together chant the passage about the newly fearless children in radiant homophony

Example 27 *Figure humaine*, p. 41, l. 1: alto part only.

rooted on C sharp major with flat seventh, the tenors and basses swaying like censers. In the bell-tolling coda and consummatory C sharp major triads man testifies to his indestructability.

A long pause is asked for, and has been earned, before the setting of the final poem, in twenty-one four-lined stanzas, each ending with the words 'J'écris ton nom'. Starting from his desk, the poet embraces the wide world—the arms of warriors and the crowns of kings, the wonders of the night, the wings of birds, the moss of clouds, the sweat of the storm, and a plethora of cosmic marvels—before returning to 'objets familiers' and the foreheads and hands of friends, whereon to write the sacred name. In the last three-stanzas particularities become abstractions: 'l'absence sans désir, la solitude nue, les marches de la mort, la santé révenue, l'espoir sans souvenir'. The question and answer form— which may have encouraged Poulenc to set the whole cantata for double choir—ends with the triumphant statement: 'Je suis né pour te connaître | Pour te nommer | LIBERTÉ'.

Musically, Poulenc starts quietly with the first choir without their basses, in triple pulse and in potentially heavenly E major. The second choir answers, 'très doux', with the refrain. Momentary modulations occur as the second choir embarks on its catalogue of places searched for and through, before appending the refrain. As the Name is sought throughout Nature and the cosmos, modulations are appropriately libertine, the two words 'ton nom' chiming like bells as the overlapping entries entangle. Tessitura rises dramatically, straining up from G sharp to B, each bar in a new key. At the climax to the catalogue the abstractions ('santé revenue, risque disparu', and so on) initiate a slight slackening of pace before the final assault, 'éclatant et très large', on B major. This is the major of the tragic B minor the cantata had

89

started from; but its grammatical function is to serve as 'enhanced dominant' to E major, in which key the work concludes. The final triad on the word 'liberté' is in 16 parts, with the basses on the E below the stave and two solo sopranos, one from each choir, on E *in alt* (above the treble stave). The effect is scalp-prickling, yet also transcendent. Despite the sophistication of Poulenc's technique, this passage has a direct impact that intensifies Renaissance idiom. In the last resort, Janus-Poulenc was not divided against himself. This was his strength, and became his country's. *Figure humaine* is an 'occasional' piece that will never lack for occasions.

3. Concerto for Organ, Strings, and Timpani (1939); Les Animaux Modèles *(1942)*

While *Figure humaine* is the apex to the evolution in Poulenc's music that began at Rocamadour, it is worth noting that the Rocamadour experience affected his instrumental as well as his vocal music. While still working on the *Litanies* and the *Motets de pénitence* Poulenc embarked on a Concerto for organ, strings, and timpani. In 1936 he wrote to the Comtesse Jean de Polignac that his concerto was 'almost complete'. In fact it wasn't finished until 1938; Francis remarked that

is has given me a lot of trouble but I hope it is all right now, and that you will like it. It is not the amusing Poulenc of the Concerto for two pianos, but more like a Poulenc en route for the cloisters, very xvth century, if you like. At Noizay I have grown into a stoutish monk, somewhat dissolute, tended by an excellent cook.

The Concerto is a deeply serious work with a disturbing amalgam of qualities, though it lacks the intensity that, in the penitential motets and in *Figure humaine*, springs from the highly charged words. Its stylistic pluralism, similar to but more perplexing than that of a work like *Concert champêtre*, embraces French traditions from the Middle Ages to the Renaissance and the baroque, affiliating Bach to French civilization in the process. Neo-classic Stravinsky is again the catalyst between the 'old' styles and the quick, balletic music in somewhat frenzied dance rhythms. War, not merely in the military sense, is in the offing, and the music, if graciously civilized, is also rather grandly redemptive. The piece may be called religious not merely because it was meant to be played in churches in preference to concert-halls.

Although the Concerto is a substantial work lasting twenty-three minutes, it plays without break, albeit in fantasia-like sectional form. Poulenc's immediate models were the quasi-improvisatory fantasias and toccatas of Buxtehude and Bach, and the adaptations of these styles made by French composers like Marchand, Gigout, and de Grigny. Poulenc opens in high baroque idiom with full-organ blazing a convoluted line in dotted rhythm over fierce chords of the tonic G minor. The first section juxtaposes this neo-baroque grandeur (and ferocity) with soft chromatic polyphony over fateful minor thirds—echoing Stravinsky's *Oedipus Rex*—on timpani and pizzicato basses. But this 'heroic' introduction ends powerfully, and is succeeded by an allegro giocoso in the style of Stravinsky's middle-period ballet music; here the panting semiquavers and jerkily syncopated melody are more frantic than jocose. The heart of the concerto is revealed in a sustained andante, wherein the organ weaves the dotted-rhythmed cantilena of the introduction into an unbroken melody in four-pulse. Tonality veers between Aeolian A minor and a pristine A major: a passage in which French baroque idiom and the neo-classic Stravinsky of his (Lullian) *Apollon Musagète* meet, creating another of Poulenc's liaisons of past with present. There's a certain unease in these equivocations between triple-rhythmed balletic elegance and duple-rhythmed martial severity, until the processional march takes over, reinstating the organ's massive introductory material, and leading to an allegro which is not a recapitulation of the first 'allegro giocoso' but an independent movement, more violent than scherzoid. Although marked 'très gai', an organ solo sounds more furious than merry, but it becomes an apotheosis when an aria is derived, 'très calme', from the introductory cantilena. The 'Apollo' theme graciously recurs, but this middle section or movement ends in the original G minor, with a coda transmuting most of the previous themes.

Both the rhythms and the tempo of the first allegro return, with the upward-thrusting scales now clearly in G major. The work seems to be coming full circle as the organ introduction is recapitulated, very loud, but suddenly becalmed in the rotating thirds. For five largo bars the organ dons Poulenc's 'antique' mantle, in sixteenth-century modality, or even in the fifteenth-century manner he surprisingly (and perhaps carelessly?) referred to in his letter to the Comtesse de Polignac. Still very soft, the organ hums the main theme, growing from the oscillating thirds and rising scale, supported by scrunchy chords over a tonic pedal (see Example 28). Strings swing in broken arpeggios, recalling the wondrous end of Stravinsky's *Symphony of Psalms*; and the concerto concludes with a reminiscence of the grand introduction, the organ thundering mordents 'à l'antique'. The ultimate end is

Example 28   Organ Concerto, p. 46, omitting first bar.

93

Example 28   *cont.*

grim as well as grand, for the timpani, having carried the aria on the fateful minor thirds, append a ferocious bump to the final orchestral unison.

It is worth noting, as an appendix to this chapter, that Poulenc's Rocamadour experience lent a darker tinge not only to his choral music and to an instrumental work for organ, but also to his theatre music. In between the Organ Concerto and the cantata *Figure humaine* Poulenc composed, in 1942, a new ballet, *Les Animaux Modèles*. That he should embark on a ballet during the German Occupation seems surprising; but dance and theatre were basic to his muse, and the task of revising his greatest success, *Les Biches*, may have persuaded him that it needed a sequel. The new ballet was produced, apparently with some éclat, at the Paris Opéra in August 1942, and Poulenc planned to offer it to Nijinska or Balanchine for production, in tandem with *Les Biches*, in America. Nothing came of these plans, and the ballet dropped out of the repertory.

As befitted the war years and the piece's proximity to the Organ Concerto and to *Figure humaine*, the appeal of *Les Animaux Modèles* is undemonstrative, compared with that of *Les Biches*. Yet it makes sense in the evolution of Poulenc's theatrical art, since in being based on the fables of La Fontaine it fuses Poulenc's preoccupation with childhood with his love of France's *grand siècle*. *Les Biches* had time-travelled between the French centuries from the sixteenth to the twentieth; *Les Animaux Modèles* is, as Francis put it, 'très Louis XIV'—to which age La Fontaine belonged, though he had been born as early as 1621, in the reign of Louis XIII. La Fontaine's wit, tenderness, and intermittent gravity have precisely the ambivalence between a mature classicism and an elegiac romanticism—looking back to the Golden Age of Louis XIII— that so entranced Poulenc in the music of Couperin. La Fontaine's fables embrace, as well as comedy and charm, ethical content, whereby human foibles and follies are tempered with irony and warmed with compassion. This steered the ballet towards Poulenc the collaborator with Eluard, rather than the young Poulenc whose literary coeval was Apollinaire—though Eluard confessed to a distaste for La Fontaine's fables, not for their literary qualities but because of the restrictive role they had played in his early education. Even so Poulenc, in between *Tel jour, telle nuit* and *Figure humaine*, discussed the new ballet with the poet, and it was Eluard who decided on a title for the piece.

The ballet comprises a number of mimed fables, the moral import of which is stressed because the beasts are 'models' with human counterparts: the cricket a frailly faded ballerina, the lion an amorous, rather ridiculous, rake, the ant an old maid from the country. Some of these animals lend themselves to satire, especially the vainglorious, love-sick lion, who shows himself off in a

Javanaise. But the two cocks, although comically illustrative like Rameau's famous 'poule', are not merely frivolous, being symbols of contradiction, associated with both treachery and dawn. This is audible in the music which, remembering *Les Biches*, quotes a real pop song of the seventeenth century.

The animal mimes have a prelude and postlude describing 'le point de jour' and 'le repos de midi'. These pieces—along with the dances associated with death, especially 'La Mort et le Bûcheron'—are fine music of which Poulenc was proud. He was distressed that his revered teacher, Charles Koechlin, considered *Les Animaux* a fall-off after *Les Biches*, admiring only its burlesque elements. It is difficult to put the ballet to the test in the theatre since it is no longer produced; concert and recorded performances, however, reveal in the dawn and midday music a sober radiance that fuses classical lucidity with a fragrant romanticism—linearly and colouristically, though not harmonically, relatable to Couperin and Rameau, while owing a direct debt to Ravel's *Daphnis et Chloé*. There is no mistaking echoes of Ravel's magical dawn-music in the slow-swinging pulse and discreetly luxuriant harmonies of Poulenc's 'point de jour' and 'repos de midi', though one recognizes the degree to which he has made them his own. Ironically, Ravel's glorious score dawned just before the First World War; Poulenc's more modest aubade glimmers in the middle of the Second, veering—as does *Figure humaine*—between violence and aspiration. It ends nobly but grimly, a paean to the precarious continuity of French civilization.

6
POULENC AU THÉÂTRE: LA CHAIR ET LE BON DIEU

1. Apollinaire and Les Mamelles de Tirésias *(1947)*

It is not surprising that, after his Rocamadour works, Poulenc felt a need for relaxation—coinciding with the end of the war, for *Figure humaine* was first performed in 1945. The cantata he believed to be his ultimate justification ('I play it every day and its underlying integrity and faith foil my foulest mood, my harshest self-criticism'). After it, he needed to unwind, and did so by returning to the theatre and to his first love, Guillaume Apollinaire: whose farce, *Les Mamelles de Tirésias*, had been written as long ago as 1903, but was not produced, with a new prologue and epilogue, until 1917—that critical year in which Francis had met the three artists to whom he owed most, Satie, Eluard, and Apollinaire himself. Poulenc set the text as an *opéra bouffe* in Offenbachian tradition, dedicating it to the composer among his friends most likely to appreciate it, Darius Milhaud. He started work on the score in 1944; its première was at the Opéra Comique on 3 June 1947. Initially a great success both critically and with the public, it has maintained a place in the repertory. No one doubted, at the time of the première, that *Les Mamelles de Tirésias*, masquerading as a product of la Belle Époque, was pertinent to social life in the late 1940s. Today, it has more specific relevance in that it deals subversively, as well as comically, with topics of gender and sexuality.

Apollinaire had set his farce in exotic Zanzibar, but Poulenc insisted that his *opéra bouffe* should take place in an imaginary town on the French Riviera—preferably resembling Monte Carlo because he (Poulenc) adored the town, and because Apollinaire had spent the first fifteen years of his life there. Monte Carlo was tropical enough for Parisian Poulenc; no doubt he also remembered that his first theatrical triumph, *Les Biches*, had been at the Monte Carlo Opera. He also backdated the action from 1917 to 1912—the 'heroic age' of Apollinaire. Time-travelling through French history is unnecessary in *Les Mamelles*; Poulenc accepts

1912 and Monte Carlo as his time and place, and notes in the score that 'sous nul prétexte la mise-en-scène ne devra être exotique'.

The action centres on a young woman, Thérèse, originally played by Denise Duval, a singer second in importance only to Bernac in Poulenc's career. Fed up with her roles as mother and household drudge, Thérèse decides to liberate herself, and to compete with men on equal terms. Opening her blouse, she allows her breasts to float off in the form of balloons. The unforeseen consequence is that she begins to sprout a beard and to acquire other male appurtenances. Transformed from Thérèse into the legendary Tirésias, she enthusiastically embarks on her 'career': which means that her husband must take over the task of continuing the human race. By mechanical means appropriate to an advanced technocracy, he manufactures 40,000 babies. The feminist trigger to the action is of course reversed in the not so long run: not because women are unjustified in seeking equality of opportunity, but because factory techniques are an inadequate substitute for sex and love.

The Prologue begins with a grandly rising triad of D minor and a fleeting glance at the double-dotted rhythm of heroic tradition. This is no more than a facetious gesture, the Second Empire parodying the first: for the orchestra dispels grandiosity with a cheeky *opéra bouffe* tune somewhere between the Dorian mode and modern D minor. The 'Directeur' addresses the audience, explaining that the piece they are about to see is meant to amuse, but also carries a moral: 'Ecoutez, O français, le leçon de la guerre et faites des enfants vous qui n'en faisiez guère'. *Les Mamelles* is a sigh, or rather giggle, of relief after the second war, as Poulenc's early frivolities had been after the first. After a passage of 'magic' Phrygian bitonality recalling the 'Western-Balinese' pattern-making in Poulenc's two-piano Concerto, the Directeur 'disparaît très lentement par une trappe'.

The curtain rises on the first scene, in which Thérèse, 'eccentrique, jeune, jolie', is cavorting around, rejecting servitude, asserting her Rights. A breathless sequence of quavers is bitonally excited by chromatics, but a lyrical tune recalls her husband's courtship of her in 'dear old Connecticut'. Perhaps Apollinaire set the wooing in the New World to explain why Thérèse had become such an 'advanced' young woman. Anyway, she has no doubt that she has seen through male chicanery and her husband's

99

in particular; and is off to be soldier, sailor, artist, lawyer, senator, President, triumphant in any profession once the prerogative of male gender. The jaunty repeated notes in the vocal line, the orchestra's flickering quaver pulse, the incessant modulations, the piquant instrumentation, add an edge of desperation to hilarity. Control breaks as her beard begins to flower and her breasts to levitate as children's balloons, climaxing in a chromatically tipsy cadenza launched from a high C. Frenzy becomes giddy joy as she dances a fast French *valse*, incipient hysteria being manifest in her coloratura's intermittent giggles and squeaks. In a gesture of defiance she bursts the balloons with her cigarette, itself a symbol of liberation, and a phallic symbol at that! She boldly accepts her male metamorphosis by transmuting her French *valse* into a darker, more macho, 'pas espagnol', in which men, hidden in the orchestral pit, reinforce her dance-song with 'Ol-lés'. At the end of the scene Thérèse-Tirésias stomps off in a 'pas militaire' to fulfil her first transvestite role as a warrior-soldier. The husband is so 'épouvanté' that he is driven into falsetto—the beginning of *his* gender-reversal.

A subsidiary theme is introduced with the appearance of M. Presto and M. Lacouf, a short fat man and a tall skinny one: 'types classiques' of French card-playing gamblers. They dance a polka which, having started blithely, touches on pathos (pentatonics and flowing parallel fourths) as they indulge in a contest of courtesy as to which has the more deplorably cheated the other at cards. Apollinaire's point, beneath the buffoonery, was perhaps to indicate that old-fashioned politesse may survive the vanity of human wishes in a society dedicated to cutthroat competition and dirty tricks. But as far as Presto and Lacouf are concerned, the gamblers' paradise is *passé*, since after a bout of idiot rhetoric they agree that honour demands a duel: in which they shoot one another dead. This doubly destructive act coincides with the reappearance of Thérèse-Tirésias, who has negated the Old World's patriarchal pride. Freshly shaven and garbed in an elegant smoking jacket, she leads in her husband in drag, his hands tied to her. Having dumped him in the café, she bounds into a dizzy patter-song about the joys of liberty and her need to be 'au fait' with the world, even to the point of buying newspapers and consorting with journalists. But an oasis of calm soothes the social romp as Thérèse, echoed by her husband and the chorus, sings—in white C major and in bland 6/8—a sad little threnody for the defunct duellists. The guileless ditty is genuinely moving, as Poulenc's model Offenbach seldom permitted himself to be. In a choral extension to the song Society itself recognizes that the duellists were casualties of a world flimsily submissive to chance. Even so, Thérèse cannot help regarding the mutually murdered males as testimony to the New World created by her liberation: 'maintenant à MOI l'univers'.

The plot thickens with the appearance of a Gendarme—another 'type classique' of French farce—mounted on a hobby-horse. As the Law, he has come to investigate the duelling deaths; but is immediately involved in the deceits of a society wherein values are stood on their heads. He makes passes at the husband, thinking him a woman; and again it is typical of Poulenc that the fake love-music is not merely risible. Meanwhile, Thérèse enacts her male roles with increasing éclat, and 'tout le monde' emulates her in role- and gender-reversal, making for chaos as well as hilarity. All the women, eschewing sex and babies, create a Lysistrata-situation. That this is not merely, if at all, a matter for mirth is evident in an entr'acte: which confronts the implications of woman's relinquishment of her procreative function in a grandly processional piece in E flat major–minor, ritualistically sung and danced by 'choristers'. This entr'acte is literally *between* worlds; the abnegation of sex may be construed as a religious act, but is in more than one sense perverse.

In any case it leads into the second act, which is a reversal of the reversal. The husband, with the help of paper, ink, glue, balloons, and scissors, has started his baby-factory. In a rampaging gallop he exhibits his synthetic 'nouveaux-nés' (who manage to pipe 'tra-la-la' refrains) to the public and an investigating journalist. He boasts of being expert at producing babies of any size, shape, or colour, and hopes that in time they—in default of a wife—will look after and support him. But he confesses that being a baby-manufacturer is a lonely occupation, and that he fears lest the proliferation of infants on an assembly-line may make for social problems. Some babies, grown up as successful painters or novelists (several topical and local jokes intrude), may threaten to take control; in any case, the sheer multiplicity of citizens is likely to create economic difficulties. So serious issues are involved in this as in most farce; and Apollinaire's response is a typically French compromise between common sense and an acceptance of human fallibility. This is why the music can be at once ludicrous and pathetic: we are prepared for the reversed reversal when Thérèse, back from her world-travels, croons to her husband a delicious little *valse* in limpid G flat major. For all the marvels she has experienced, she's left with the admission that, without love (and sex), she must 'succombe avant ce rideau tombe'.

So 'le mari' resumes his male attire and the crowd, the newspaper man, and vicariously the audience join in a choric dance. The *valse* becomes a farcical buffo finale, incorporating an appeal to everybody to 'faire des enfants', regardless of size, shape, or colour. It is not clear what happens to the multitudinous fabricated babies, but flesh and blood people may decide that they were as illusory as Thérèse's breast-balloons. Poulenc's stage-direction leaves no further need for words: 'Les femmes se blottissent amoureusement contre les hommes.' The final cadence displaces the opera's original modal D minor with earthy F major—with oddly satisfying effect, given that tonality has throughout been as ephemeral as our social conventions. Perhaps it was *Les Mamelles*'s unabashed effrontery in respect, or disrespect, of those conventions that so endeared the work to its composer. Writing to his biographer Henri Hell in 1953 he exclaimed that it was 'definitely the work that is dearest to me, that at heart I prefer to all others. See how alive the orchestration is, how clear and varied it sounds, and how the vocal parts stand out well. . . . Perhaps the heart of the matter is that the worst of myself is the best of myself.' Although there was a sense in which Poulenc truly believed this, he none the less complained with increasing frequency that he resented being known mainly for his *jeux d'esprit*, rather than for the *Motets pour un temps de pénitence*, for *Figure humaine*, or for his 'grand' opera, *Dialogues des Carmélites*. Ultimately, he loved his 'commonness' because he knew it was the fundament from which he was able, occasionally, to become a great composer.

2. Bernanos and Dialogues des Carmélites (1953–1957)

Les Mamelles de Tirésias, Poulenc's first opera, was and is physically life-enhancing. *Dialogues des Carmélites* is metaphysically death-celebrating, and forms a complement, as well as polar opposite, to *Les Mamelles*. By far his longest work, it came 'out of the blue' in that Signor Valcarenghi, then employed by Poulenc's current publisher Ricordi, secured for the composer a commission from La Scala, Milan. The original idea was for a ballet on the life of Santa Margherita of Cortona; but Poulenc retorted that, if he were to write something for La Scala, it should surely be a grand opera. Valcarenghi suggested that Georges Bernanos's play about nuns victimized in the French Revolution would be a likely subject: an inspired choice, for both the theme and the powerful simplicity of Bernanos's language offered Francis a chance to explore afresh the religious impulses that had motivated the penitential motets and to relate—as in *Figure humaine*—eternal spiritual themes to topically political events. For the French Revolution was a victory for secularism, in the wake of which we still live. Modern life and Old France could coexist; and, as in the case of the *Motets pour un temps de pénitence*, Poulenc had a private motive that focused the public one. During the early 1950s he hovered on the edge of another breakdown, occasioned by his lacerating love affair with a young man called Lucien Roubert. Probably it was only Bernac's calm solicitude and moral steadfastness that steered Francis through anguish that Bernac considered self-indulgent to the point of lunacy. None the less Poulenc, tougher than he seemed, survived, writing his sacrificial opera while Lucien laboured under a distressing terminal illness.

The case of *Dialogues des Carmélites* suggests that, if private anguish was an impulse to creation, salvation accrued from the very process of composition. Repeatedly during his first month's work on the opera Poulenc wrote to his friends of the fervour that possessed him: to Bernac, 'I have begun *Les Carmélites* and literally *cannot sleep* because of it!'; to Stéphane Audel, 'I am working like a *madman*, I do not go out, I do not see anyone . . . I do not want to think of anything else . . . I am completing one scene a week. I am crazy about my subject, to the point of believing that I have actually known these women'; to Bernac again, 'It just flows and flows, and it is like nobody but myself. It is madly vocal. I check each note and am careful to place the right vowels on the high notes. Not to mention the prosody: I do believe that every word will be understood.' To Rose Darcourt-Plaut he wrote that 'I do not think I have ever done anything as good. You will see— it is terrifying. When I play it to you, you will weep and weep.' He adds that he is no longer the 'demented wreck' that he was last summer, in the depths of his abyss over Lucien; and that the completion of the opera coincident with the boy's death surely argued some kind of divine cognizance. 'I got up from my table and said to my faithful Anna: "I have finished. Monsieur Lucien will die now". Who will ever know all that lies at the secret heart of certain works?'

The kind of opera Poulenc created was naturally conditioned by the text. Bernanos's play had been freely based on a short novel by Gertrude von le Fort, which was in turn founded on a true story. Since Bernanos's text was poetically incandescent, Poulenc believed that in being faithful to it he would be faithful to himself. It follows that his opera has no connection with the soli-and-ensemble structure of romantic Italian opera and virtually no link with Wagnerian music-drama, except in so far as he uses musical 'images' that might be related to leitmotives. Poulenc's *Les Carmélites* harks back to the Monteverdian concept of a play in music, scrupulously faithful to the nuances of the text, which are emotionally intensified, but not radically changed, by the score. The only later parallels are with the operas of Moussorgsky, whose relationship to Poulenc as a composer of childhood we have briefly touched on; and with Debussy's *Pelléas et Mélisande*, an almost verbatim setting of Maeterlinck's play. Poulenc's opera is, however, more traditional in that it preserves affinities with classical French theatre-music from Lully to Rameau, and embraces echoes of Gluck, Berlioz, Bizet, Massenet, Chabrier, and the Fauré of *Pénélope*. Poulenc's respect for Bernanos's text safeguards him from eclecticism; Albert Béguin, testamentary of Bernanos, admired the way in which Poulenc had 'remained absolutely faithful to the main lines of a very delicate architecture . . . I rediscover *all* of Bernanos in your presentation'. Complementarily, the Abbé Daniel Pézeril, Bernanos's confessor, thanked Poulenc for having found his way 'into the very heart of the *Dialogues*—a meeting of souls if ever there were one'.

Monteverdi, speaking of his *Orfeo*, said that it mated recitative, which is speaking while singing, with arioso, which is singing while speaking. This applies to Poulenc's opera which, given his empathy with the human voice and his command of French prosody, relates character both to the inner life of the psyche and to action in the world. Bernanos's play has a singular intensity; in dividing it into three acts in twelve tableaux—with a number of interludes either purely orchestral or played in front of the curtain—Poulenc produced an opera libretto of comparable trenchancy, making his music revelatory of, yet subservient to, the dramatic effect. Much of the work is thinly scored, and the large orchestral forces are lavishly employed only in explicitly symphonic interludes and in the great final scene.

The first tableau offers information and psychological evidence on which the drama will depend. We are in the old, aristocratic world, in the library of the Marquis de la Force. But the date is April 1789: so it is appropriate that the pompously rhythmed, grandly dissonant introduction, with its overt references to French baroque music, should lead into a scene in which the open sevenths and spacious textures are exacerbated by nervously repeated thirds, hinting at the threat to which the Old France is exposed (see Example 29). This Old World theme will recur in sundry guises, both positive and negative in effect, throughout the opera.

Example 29 *Dialogues des Carmélites*: Act 1, tableau 1: p. 1, l. 3.

The action starts when the Chevalier awakens his father from a snooze (which makes a point about him and history) in the entrenched and codified past of his library. Father and son, conversing, introduce the opera's basic theme in both its private and its public manifestations. They are worried about the Marquis's daughter (and Chevalier's sister) Blanche who, nervously distressed, threatens withdrawal from a world she cannot cope with. The Marquis pooh-poohs her anguish as a mild attack of 'nerves' easily cured by a sound marriage; but the Chevalier, more in tune with what's happening in the world, suspects that her malaise is, like that of society, deep-seated. That the personal crisis is related to public events is underlined by their talk of unrest among infuriated peasants; and we can appreciate Poulenc's partiality for his text if we note the parallels between his own crisis and those of his operatic creatures. Loving Old France, Poulenc had something of the Marquis in him, while being also a 'modern', like the Chevalier. At the same time, hating many qualities of the contemporary world, he was prone to nervous maladjustments similar to those of Blanche, especially in the dark light of his earlier crisis of faith and his current affair with Lucien. What is remarkable is the way in which this opening scene, purveying information by way of dialogue and description, defines so many of the dramatic and musical roots of the whole opera. Wavering diatonic concords in false relation suggest both social instability and Blanche's lost state (see Example 30); a double-dotted figure thrusting up through a third, accompanied by a chromatically undulating bass, offers threat both physical and metaphysical, but may also suggest fortitude (see Example 31). These and many other motives will be subjected to sundry metamorphoses as the action unfolds.

At a crucial point during their conversation Blanche timidly joins her father and brother in the library. The Chevalier welcomes her as his 'petit lièvre', a childhood endearment that may

Example 30 *Dialogues des Carmélites*: Act 1, tableau 1: p. 4, l. 2, bars 2–3.

Le C.

a   du re-brous-ser   che - min,   deux   fois,

pp

Example 31 *Dialogues des Carmélites*: Act 1, tableau 1: p. 4, l. 1, bars 1–2.

bear on her diffidence in addressing the world. She reprimands him for what she sees as condescension, informing him that she is not so much frightened of the mob that lusts for aristocratic blood as undermined by obscure fears that allow her no peace in the world she belongs to. The scene takes place more or less at the speed of speech, yet its realism plumbs minds and senses. Another musical 'image'—a fluctuation of sequential sevenths as well as of diatonic concords—becomes the most pervasive motif of the opera (see Example 32), for it is a double aural image befitting a double man or woman. The chords' unrelatedness, and the *false* relations endemic to them, suggest a lack of centre and of the direction inherent in tonal progression. Yet at the same time this lost condition, oblivious of the way of the world, has a positive aspect in so far as a deficiency in 'will' may indicate a need to be released from it, to substitute metaphysical for physical satisfactions. In that sense the motif may be associated with holy matters: an affiliation not unprecedented, since concordant but unrelated triads, usually in root position, were common in the liturgical music of the Renaissance—God's music at a time when a theocratic world was being humanistically transmuted.

Even at this early stage in the opera it is clear that Blanche's terror of the world is not a mere negation. Danger, she says, may act like a *douche* of cold water, making one more rather than less aware. Evidence is immediately proferred, for she asks permission to retire to her room, where she will be screened from the contagion of the world. Her brother advises her to provide herself with candles as assurance against the fearsome dark; and proves to have a point, since she utters a sudden yell of alarm, occasioned not by a ghost but by the unexpected appearance of Thierry, the Marquis's valet: a palpable working man, and an emissary from the

Example 32 *Dialogues des Carmélites*: Act 1, tableau 1: p. 18, bottom line (with voice).

minatory 'real' world. Throughout the scene the music interlaces contradictory but complementary dramatic themes: the Old World motif the opera had started from; the falsely related concords that apply alike to Blanche's neurasthenia and to social unease; and forebodings of the minor thirds of the epilogic funeral march. Moreover, this opening scene, although expository, attains a genuine climax when Blanche sings to her father an arioso—it almost amounts to an aria—about submission to God's will as the only source of tranquility of soul. Her song is in regular four-pulse over tonic pedal notes on G, traditionally a key of benediction. Both pulse and vocal line are unbroken even, or especially, when she confesses that she wishes to take the veil. Although the Marquis finds this difficult to sympathize with, or even to comprehend, he seems, after protest, to agree that she should be responsible for herself. Yet Poulenc's music reveals how difficult self-responsibility must be for a young girl so entwined in familial ties: which is why her chaste arioso swells into almost operatically lyrical passion, or at least into melodies comparable with Poulenc's songs of the war years. The wide-ranging lines combine with flatward-tending modulations and with Poulenc's typical syncopated accompanying figures simultaneously to suggest anxiety and fortitude. Rising minor thirds are recurrent in the bass, hinting—though we cannot yet know this—at Blanche's destiny. Circuitously, she finds a way home to a high G sharp on the word 'honneur', the G sharp being the third of a dominant ninth of A minor. In this basic key the Old World motif sings 'infiniment doux', and twice as slow. The last sounds of the scene are the funeral minor thirds on timpani.

The second scene takes place 'quelques semaines après' in the Carmelite convent of Compiègne, where Blanche has come to consult the Prioress about her admission to the Order. The orchestral prelude evokes the Old World, though, given the religious ambience, its tone is severe rather than grand. Even the baroque double-dotted rhythm is hardly resplendent, for its key is dark B flat minor. In this scene the darkness is specifically that of the Old Prioress, who is ill unto death; her acerbity, assertive of the Order's rigour, is pathologically intensified by her consciousness of mortality. If Blanche is terrified of the chaos endemic in the outside world, the Old Prioress is no less shattered within walls that had once afforded solace. Poulenc finds a powerful musical image for the confrontation between the young and the old woman: a sequence of slow triplets in G minor, with the funereal minor thirds implacable in the bass. In arioso the Prioress tells Blanche first of her own infirmities, then of the necessity, imposed by the Order, to achieve freedom from the selfhood she has just manifested. She challenges Blanche's youthful unpreparedness in recitative of formidable trenchancy. Poulenc's claim to have devised a 'madly vocal' idiom so attuned to French prosody that 'every word will be understood' is justified, as is his claim to have respected the relationships between vocal resource and character. Blanche's young, sometimes tremulous, soprano is in psychological as well as musical tension with the Prioress's rasping, sometimes cavernous, mezzo, both being parts that offer rewards commensurate with their challenges. Yet despite the tension between the two women, they are bonded; this is manifest at the end of the scene when the Prioress momentarily drops her guard to admit that the convent is justified only as a house of prayer. A moment of 'très intense' arioso in heavenly E major epitomizes this, and leads into an epilogue wherein Blanche asks that her conventual name be Blanche of the Agony of Christ on the Cross. Such had been the Prioress's religious name on her initiation; and we'll discover that Blanche's agony, in spiritual if not physical terms, complements that of the dying woman—both musically evident in falsely related concords and sevenths. The Prioress closes the interview by blessing the novice in a grandly fierce rising fifth and falling sixth: after which the orchestra returns to the G minor triplet figuration of the opening of the scene, with deathly minor thirds in the bass. Yet the final chord is a luminously spaced G *major* triad: which offers hope of redemption for young Blanche, who will eventually die the 'good death' denied to the Prioress.

The next tableau is separated from the hermetic confrontation between Blanche and the Prioress by an orchestral interlude, busily reminding us of the world outside the convent. It concludes, however, with a canonic passage for brass, in which modal alterations hint, in Stravinskian style, at medieval austerity. Within the walls, 'busy-ness' is not abated, as the curtain rises on the nuns' morning routine. Blanche, young herself, chats with a 'très jeune' nun, pointedly called Constance. The music–allegro in a perky A minor–majorish 2/4—recalls the youthful Poulenc we are familiar with, telling us that convent life isn't exclusively a matter of prayer and purgatory. But we cannot describe the scene as light relief, for it offers another strand in the tangle of human motives. After Blanche and the Old Prioress, Constance is the most significant character in the opera, since her child-like innocence is to prove the agent of Blanche's belated redemption. The psychological interplay explored by Bernanos thus accords with the theme latent throughout Poulenc's works: as becomes explicit here, when the girls' idle chatter unexpectedly embraces first and last things. Blanche reproves Constance for joking whilst the Prioress is dying: to which the young girl retorts that her pleasure in childish things does no one harm, and that there is nothing she could do for one so old—no less than 59! Constance even queries whether Blanche, whom she reveres as well as loves, is not unconsciously bent on doing her harm; and seems to have a point when Blanche contemptuously, and perhaps jealously, rejects Constance's invitation to pray with her as 'un enfantillage'. In relation to Constance, Blanche is here what the Prioress was to herself in the previous scene, and of the two the 'child' Constance is the stronger. Blanche, subconsciously knowing this, says that she *envies* Constance's simplicity—patent in the dancing octaves and sixths in her vocal line, fraily supported by unrelated concords and sevenths. Such music offers a more positive metamorphosis of Blanche's dubieties; but in immediate context Blanche (from a high B) dismisses Constance's 'idée folle et stupide' that she will die young, her destiny mystically linked with that of a loved friend. 'Très poignant et doux', Constance murmurs 'j'étais bien loin de vouloir vous offenser': which is true indeed, and a measure of the gulf between Blakean innocence and experience. In the last three bars F major shifts, or is forcibly wrenched, to a fortissimo A minor triad, returning the convent to the context of the harsh world.

Again turbulence in the world is identified with turmoil within the mind. After a riotous orchestral interlude dominated by clangorous convent bells—punning on tritonal fifths in the Lydian mode and perfect fifths in B minor—the climactic scene of the act is at the Old Prioress's deathbed. Her monologue is as terrifying as Poulenc said it was: so much so that we cannot doubt that it mirrors his own agony of doubt and the fear of death he had experienced vicariously through Lucien. The Prioress's monologue begins 'très calme' in 3/4, over an orchestral motif of rocking octaves almost identical with the piano figuration in the first number of *Tel jour, telle nuit*. The quaver octaves are a clock that remorselessly ticks away time, but also a beating heart that tries to hold pulse and pitch while the orchestra's chords chromatically disintegrate. The Prioress chides her own helplessness in the face of pain, resisting attempts at consolation from Mère Marie, the Assistant Prioress. As the rocking octaves are metamorphosed into devilish tritones she snarls that her lot must be to watch herself die. Here both the pantingly syncopated quavers and the double-dotted thrust up a third imbue the recitative with a passion that stresses its root meaning of suffering. Intermittently, the octaves return at various pitches. The Prioress complains that Blanche, though summoned to the deathbed, has not appeared; and to increasingly tormented music she senses a kinship between the agony of her death and that of Blanche's doubt. She commits Blanche to Mère Marie's care after she, the Prioress, is dead. Her savage line is bolstered by orchestral dissonances and the familiar G minor thirds.

As Blanche belatedly enters, in fear and trembling, the double-dotted rising third and the chromatically wriggling bass accompany her as she kneels, to chromatically dissolving strings marked pppp, at the bedside. The dying woman pleads in agitated syncopations, for the relief that only the doctor's drugs can now offer. Losing control, she denies God in wildly leaping arioso: 'Que suis-je à cette heure, moi misérable, pour m'inquiéter de Lui. Qu'il s'inquiète donc d'abord de moi!' She collapses, and 'on entend son râle'. The rest of the horrifying scene, from which the hedonistic Poulenc never flinches, consists of semi-articulate cries from the Prioress, injected into appalled recitative from Mère Marie, while Blanche is stunned to silence and the orchestra transforms its growling semitones into the fateful G minor thirds. Significantly, when the Prioress momentarily recovers articulacy sufficient to upbraid God for having forsaken her, it is to the unrelated concords, now fortissimo, that had been associated with Blanche's hysteria (see Example 33). After the dying woman's denial of God the tumult of the convent bells identifies inner anguish with outer chaos; the minor thirds, thudding down the scale from A to the E flat a tritone apart, are hideously reinforced by the Prioress's death-rattle. A suddenly calm epilogue swings from B minor to rocking thirds between E and G, through which Blanche stands petrified while Mère Marie, a voice of sense and sanity, asks God to forgive the Reverend Mother for her 'peur de la mort'. The Prioress shrilly echoes, almost parodies, the phrase as she in fact 'tombe morte'. In a coda based on her fluctuating seventh chords Blanche stammers that she thinks the Reverend Mother was trying to say something; but since she is no more capable of articulacy than the Prioress, the act ends on an unanswered question—Blanche's, as well as the Prioress's. During a slow curtain a convent bell resounds through a B minor triad: traditionally a key of suffering, most sublimely in Bach and Couperin.

The end of the Old Prioress's reign concludes the first stage of Blanche's pilgrimage. Bernanos's play now asks whether her destiny must echo that of the Prioress of the Agony of Christ, or whether she may yet find salvation *through* Christ. An answer is implicit in the opening of the second act, for Blanche is on watch, *with Constance*, by 'le corps de la défunte'. The music begins in

Example 33 *Dialogues des Carmélites*: Act 1, tableau 4: p. 92, l. 1, last bar, and l. 2, bars 1–3.

the antique manner of the Organ Concerto, in three-part canon on a baroque-style motif incorporating a demisemiquaver flourish. The young women chant, in Latin, fragments of the Requiem liturgy; in a seraphic Amen Blanche, though lower in pitch, shares in Constance's radiance, cadencing in innocent A major (see Example 34). But when Blanche, left alone, tries to pray, she fails—to fragmented F minor tritones! The orchestra attempts, unsuccessfully, to resume the noble incantation of the act's opening, and Mère Marie, again counselling respect for human limitation, advises Blanche that a second attempt at prayer would be impotent; better not to brood on failure, but to seek the solace of sleep. Marie's recitative is accompanied by a harmonic ostinato similar to

Example 34 *Dialogues des Carmélites*: Act 2, tableau 1: p. 100, bottom line (voice and piano).

Blanche's oscillating concords, at first irresolute, but growing forceful to culminate in clashes of minor and major third at the very moment when she advocates the balm of sleep. Poulenc had complained to Bernac, in the early days of work on the opera, that Mère Marie was the only character he couldn't get the measure of. By this time he would seem to be fully in command; his Marie is a good woman who, in Hardy's phrase, 'did good things'—a realist and empiricist. In this context her point would seem to be that, just as death had, for the Prioress, opened a Pandora's box of horrors, so sleep carries the possibility of nightmare. None the less it may also have therapeutic potential; and her harmonic ostinato turns benign as she asks for God's blessing on them all, as a new day dawns. The convent bells may have jarred out of tune, as they had at the moment of the Prioress's fearful end; but the orchestral postlude not only returns 'fièrement' to the organ-style canon, it also resolves into vernal A major.

   This is an appropriate introduction to the next interlude, which again brings together the crucial duo of Blanche and Constance, who are literally making crosses of flowers, to adorn the Prioress's hearse. They discuss the Prioress's possible successor, Blanche with suspicion, Constance with perhaps gullible candour. Constance thinks that Mère Marie should succeed to the office—an instinctively wise choice in view of Marie's respect for the mean. Blanche disagrees, perhaps because she suspects that Marie's common sense might be insufficiently indulgent of neurotic distress. Constance finds it difficult to believe that the Prioress made so bad an end, and touchingly wonders whether it may not have been God's fault: he must have got muddled and allotted her the death intended for some less holy person. Funereal minor thirds are obsessive in this seriously whimsical passage, at first in the opera's (and 'reality's') basic A minor, but shifting to C minor (the key of the Prioress's death and of Blanche's), and to dark B flat minor (a key later associated negatively with revolutionary violence and positively with the New Prioress). So even this apparently slight episode has its place in the opera's scheme: as becomes patent when Constance elevates speech-like recitative to child-like song as she floats octaves and sixths above a pendulum of alternating major thirds and sevenths chords. When she adds that some people's deaths could be as easy as the Old Prioress's was hard, she reaches the redemptive heart of Bernanos's play: 'on ne meurt pas chacun pour soi, mais les uns pour les autres, ou même les uns à la place des autres. Qui sait?' Her rising sixth on the question hangs in the air, colouring what is to come. The interlude—which we have seen to be far from interludial—ends off-key, sliding from A minor with flat seventh to a triad of D sharp minor, a tritone apart.

The next tableau is set in the convent chapel, where the 'religieuses' are assembled to take a vow of obedience to the New Prioress, Mère Marie de St. Augustine. That her name is Marie suggests that she shares some of the Assistant Prioress's unaffected humanity, while that she is associated with St Augustine could point to a lively awareness of guilt. The orchestral prelude, in 3/4 at walking pace, is without rhythmic perturbation, as though to affirm the continuity of unalterable law; yet, being in B flat minor, the music remains death-tinged, albeit not direfully, since the stepwise-moving lines are not strictly in B flat minor, but rather in the Aeolian mode on B flat. Occasionally the level flow is ruffled by a shift from diatonic scale-movement to whole tones, hinting at the disembodiment typical of Satie's 'Rose-Croix' musics (see Example 35). That leaves their fate in the lap of God, if not the gods: a point which the New Prioress makes explicitly, when she tells her children that they must be content with small mercies, and with the knowledge that the courage of simple

Example 35 *Dialogues des Carmélites*: Act 2, tableau 2: p. 113, top line.

women is not inferior to that of kings and princes. The texture of stepwise-moving parts changes to broken arpeggios over rock-like pedal notes on D, with many of the opera's basic motives woven into the inner parts. Mère Marie thanks the New Prioress for her unaffected testament and invites the nuns to kneel in prayer. The scene ends with their chanting an Ave Maria in three-part organum in a quasi-pentatonic A major. The Amen, in the manner of Poulenc's motets, is 'out of this world', but the orchestral postlude anneals modal ambiguity in favour of F sharp minor: a key which, being B minor's dominant, in baroque music often implied heightened suffering. There are sundry emotional ambiguities here, associated with the fact that the Prioress has to leave her 'children', at their moment of trial, to go on a mission to Paris. This may mean that a crisis-situation permits of no alternative; or that the Prioress herself cannot face the terror of the moment; or that the nuns need to confront their ultimate test alone.

At this point a frenetic interlude, again in dark B flat minor, offers assault on religious hermitage from the world outside. Poulenc displays theatrical instinct in tempering threat with relief: for the hammering on the gates is not what we expect. Far from being a revolutionary rabble, the intruder is the old world in the person of the Chevalier, who has come to lure Blanche away from the convent to what he hopes, against the odds, might be the safety of home. The violence of the music is explained by the fact that the old world's seductiveness cannot but perturb Blanche in being illusory; certainly this third tableau intensifies the seductions the past had offered her in the first act. The confrontation of brother and sister induces passionate music, using the adjective not as a synonym for suffering, but in its modern sense. Indeed, the sustained lyrical flow suggests the operatic love-music of Massenet, though there is a harder edge to its poignancy. The key of C sharp minor usually promises serious passion in Poulenc and here the vocal lines, supported by the familiar pulsing quavers, approximate to the more emotive *mélodies* of the war years. Woven into the love-music are most of the opera's pervasive motives: the double-dotted rising thirds, indicative of both nobility and tension; the semitonically wriggling bass; and the Old World motif that had launched the opera, now translated into lyrical, but declining, sequences, as the Chevalier portrays the Marquis alone among his frightened servants, and woos Blanche with memories of childhood and youth (see Example 36). Although the scene is about division and contradiction, with Blanche torn between the sensuous security of home and lonely subservience to what she believes to be the will of God, Poulenc maintains momentum, perhaps because his heroine's crisis is so deeply involved with his own.

Example 36 *Dialogues des Carmélites*: Act 2, tableau 3: p. 134, ll. 1 and 2.

cont.

Example 36 *Cont.*

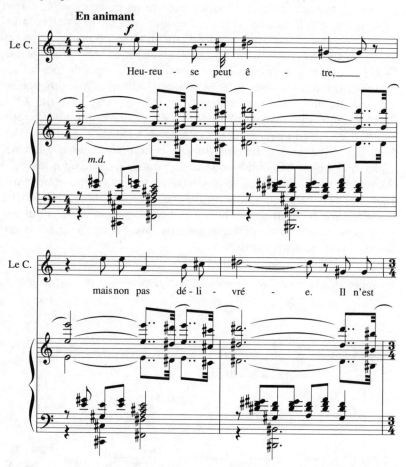

Admitting, in the simplest procession of major triads, that Blanche seems to have conquered her fears, the Chevalier agrees to leave her in the convent—only to be hysterically summoned back by his sister in a molto agitato return to C sharp minor and the double-dotted rhythm of the love-duet. She seems to be trying to transmute her love-music into a paean to God, for whom they must both do battle after their own fashions. Yet when the Chevalier has left, Blanche admits to commonsensical Mère Marie that she had almost succumbed to his *temptations*, and now doesn't know where she stands in relation to the sacred and the profane. There is a significant recurrence of the grinding major–minor thirds provoked, at the wake, by her inability to pray. Mère Marie is once more on the mark in reminding Blanche that hers is the ultimate sin of pride. But the orchestral postlude transforms the Old World theme into potential heroism, with trumpet defining E flat triads over a deep pedal C. The music's ambivalence mirrors that of the pained protagonists, including Poulenc himself.

In the next tableau threat to the convent's sanctity is more brutal, having nothing to do with the lure of an aristocratic past. But it is still not the ultimate confrontation of past with present, but is rather a disintegration from within—inevitable, given the tide of events. The scene is the sacristy of the convent, and the music opens with the familiar A minor thirds, pounding beneath a wailing chromatic lament. The Almoner of the Order tells the nuns that he has celebrated the last Mass permitted him. His moderate-paced arioso is sober, for as a man of God it is his duty to override temporal distraction. But his song is 'mélancolique' in impotence, at least until he leads the nuns in chanting a three-part Ave Maria. This is a more positive permutation of similar passages in the Prioress's death-scene and in *Tel jour, telle nuit*, and it has different effects on different members of the community. The Almoner decides that, to save the Church, he must needs go into hiding; Constance berates the world (including the Almoner?) for its craven failure to defend the faith; Blanche— 'd'une voix presque sans timbre'—confesses that her fear is 'une maladie' with which she cannot cope. But everyone is fortified by the double-dotted thirds winding into the wavering sevenths, and the Prioress, 'très calme' over level pedal notes on F, reminds her flock that it is not for them to decide whether they will be crowned with martyrdom.

For the moment of truth is at hand: the hubbub at the gates is now the revolutionary rabble itself. Ferocious trumpet fanfares pierce the texture as the rabble leaders demand that the convent gates be unbarred. Eventually, Marie accedes, and the rout tumbles through the doors in a vividly physical image of descending tritones in dotted rhythm—almost a literal inversion of a conventional metaphor for aristocratic heroism—now raucously fortissimo, in infernal F minor. Over an ostinato of pedal notes the Commissioner proclaims the new state law rendering religious communities illegal. Fluctuating triads in false relation powerfully reflect both devotion and dubiety, while the Commissioner barks a low vaudeville ditty, in the music-hall manner of *Le Bal masqué*, now sneerily grotesque rather than jovial. In this context such music is unequivocal negation—though the Commissioner claims that he is not such a thug as his mates. He is not unsympathetic to the Church, but of course, and all too familiarly, he has no choice but to obey orders and 'howl with the other wolves'.

His crude oompah basses momentarily give way to the nuns' falsely related concords as he promises to help them escape, while also warning them of a blacksmith informer, ironically called Blancard, who is to prove their undoing. But possibly his name is not ironic, since it is related to white Blanche, and the sisters' ultimate salvation is their maryrdom. However this may be, salvation is not yet; and there is the bitterest irony in the fact that, after the commissioners have left, Mère Jeanne hands Blanche a clay figure of the infant Jesus, for this day of wrath is also Christmas Eve! Blanche exclaims piteously at the child-god's tininess and frailty and, scared by the yelling rabble outside, drops him on the stone floor. God is shattered, and his remnants are obliterated by the nasty new world as a raucous little military march (marked 'très gai!') is blared outside in a (now ruthless) B flat minor, while the mob bellows 'Ah! ça ira'.

Through the first two acts Poulenc has achieved a cumulative marriage of music and theatre, from the expository early scenes to the conflicts between forces sacred and profane, to the physical confrontation between convent and rabble. His ultimate task is the resolution of conflict in spiritual transcendence—and specifically in the salvation of the young woman whose crisis so closely parallels his own. Grandeur is potent in the opening of the third act, which begins in the convent chapel, now despoiled by the mob. The orchestral prelude—at Tempo de Sarabande, though the time signature veers between 3/4 and 4/4—reflects the one-time or potential holy truth of Old France, while at the same time revealing the nobility that even the frailest heart may aspire to. The majesty of French baroque pervades the double-dotted rhythm as the theme, marked 'fièrement', swells from the rising third motif, initially in the Aeolian mode on A, the fundamental tonality of the opera. Leaping octaves in the inner parts remind us of those in the Prioress's death-scene and in *Tel jour, telle nuit*; but the music opens up to absorb the religious rather than secular grandeur of the prelude to the second act, garlanded with baroque flourishes. Previously, the bass had been riddled with tritones; now the harmony is at first pure Aeolian, shifting to C sharp minor in recollection of the love-duet.

The sweep of the musical paragraphs is unbroken as Mère Marie asks the Almoner to address the nuns about their vow to accept martydrom rather than accede to the tenets of the Revolution. When he suggests that she would be a more appropriate intermediary, she sings in speech rhythms, over an ostinato of fluctuating chords similar to, but with more tonal direction than, Blanche's vacillating sevenths. She ends on an ostinato on B, with the double-dotted rising thirds here instilling fortitude. Mère Jeanne—whose modest place in the pattern we may now appreciate—voices common fallibility when she complains that so many 'special' vows may lead to doubt about their interpretation. Mère Marie counters this by insisting that openness of choice is the heart of the matter. The noble sarabande theme is in hopefully rising sequences though, in music related to Blanche's ambivalences, she says she would abandon the vow, were there but one dissenting voice. She suggests that they should decide the issue by secret ballot; and while the vote is cast, the music changes from the grandeur of the opening of the act into wildly modulatory music that is heroic but tormented, with the baroque demisemiquaver 'flourish' now more savage than civilized. Stray nuns mutter that there is bound to be one abstainer, meaning Blanche. So there is; but Constance, protecting her idol, pretends that the defector is herself—only to change her mind, perhaps in youthful timidity, perhaps in the hope that Blanche will follow suit. To pulsing chords the Almoner asks the two youngest nuns, Constance and Blanche, to affirm their vow on the Holy Book. After they have done so, an orchestral postlude reasserts the noble sarabande theme in F sharp minor—cataclysmically answered, in 'lugubre' F minor, by the deathly minor thirds. But the final chord, though very short, is major; the whole passage tonally epitomizes the emotional ambiguities that are the opera's essence.

In an interlude, in front of the curtain, we find the Carmelites imprisoned by the secular State. A dreary monotone of quavers in the Phrygian mode accompanies an archaic, pentatonic-Aeolian melody on oboe, mourning their fate. The flavour of the music is antique, almost medieval, as though the sisters have indeed been left behind by Time. When an Officer of the Law enters and obsequiously congratulates them on their public spirit, the regular pulse does not change, though the harmonies grow more earthy and the organum effects may even suggest parody of nunnish music. He informs the sisters that they must appear individually before a state tribunal, and may generously be allowed to live a new life of liberty 'sous la surveillance des Lois'. When the officers leave, the Prioress exhorts the nuns to courage, concluding in an arioso 'très calme et ineffablement doux', over arpeggios of B flat. That this lyrical peroration is in or around B flat minor suggests that the forces of evil may be countered by brave women no less than by men. That some people find courage a difficult goal is, however, patent, for the next tableau is set in the library of the Marquis's ancestral home, where the action of the opera had started and where Blanche, too craven to sustain her vow, has taken refuge, 'vêtue comme une femme du peuple'.

The Marquis has been a victim of the guillotine and Blanche seems to be hiding incognito with the remnants of the household servants, whom she herself now serves. Unsurprisingly the action-music, after a solemn orchestral prelude, opens in the F minor the previous scene had ended in, its dotted rhythms now distraught rather than heroic. Mère Marie enters, attempting to persuade Blanche to return to the convent. In pitifully agitated recitative Blanche confesses that she is too terror-stricken to leave, and thinks nowhere could be safer than her dead father's house, where her enemies would never think of looking for her. Unable to distinguish between moral issues and trivialities, she hysterically upbraids Marie for causing her to burn the soup she is heating; and tries to defend herself on the grounds that she has been terrified all her life, and in the eye of God fear is no more than a venal sin. The thunderous minor thirds of death alternate with recollections of Old World music associated with the father she had loved, and the heroic motif of the opera's first bars sighs in heart-rending sequences. Marie, giving Blanche time to summon courage, leaves her with the address of a religious friend to whom she should repair, to be called for by Marie in the morning. Blanche protests that she is unready for the test; Marie says she must be. The music fluctuates violently between the noble sarabande motives and the dotted-rhythmed F minor of Blanche's frenzy. A cracked bell tolls as a voice from the kitchen summons Blanche, a servant in her own home, to menial chores.

The third tableau happens at dawn, which is a new day, though the setting is the state prison, where the Carmelites are incarcerated. The Prioress, who has returned from her visit to Paris, sings to her children, assuring them, 'très doux et calme', that the first night of ordeal is the worst. Now, they are ready for transcendence, should it occur. The music is in the purgatorial key of E minor—for Bach a key of crucifixion—with a quaver pulse as regular as a heart-beat and a long, winding theme that seems to be a distillation of all the positive motives of the opera. The Prioress's song is not arioso but fully fledged aria, certainly noble, perhaps sublime; after a modulation to the dominant, it climaxes in traditionally celestial E major, embracing, moreover, the heroic double-dotted figures that had been associated with the old world. It would seem that the New Prioress is a redemptive agent, or angel, who atones for the dubieties of Blanche and even of the Old Prioress; in any case she, who had missed the vow-taking through whatever motive or lack of one, now herself takes the vow of martyrdom, as the grand sarabande theme sails over a D major pedal. She forgives herself, the Old Prioress, and humankind in reminding her flock that Christ himself, on the Mount of Olives, 'a eu peur de la mort'. The key teeters between pastoral F major and tenebrous B flat minor; and the interdependence of light and dark is further pointed when Constance interrupts the devotions to ask what will happen to absent Blanche. The Prioress says that only God knows, but Constance is convinced that she does too, for that Blanche will return has been revealed to her in a dream. Her lovely phrase, modulating from light A major back to black F minor, elicits a nervous giggle from the other, especially older, nuns; but the Gaoler, roughly bursting in, negates the majestic serenity of the Prioress's aria, as well as the nuns' uneasy mirth.

He shouts on repeated notes between E and G—minor thirds in the context of an F minor diminished seventh, 'horrendous' in both key and chord. In rapid *parlando* he barks a roll-call of the nuns' names, reducing them to ciphers. Sickening oompah basses cease only when he pronounces sentence of death on all these Enemies of the People, the Revolution, and the New State. As accompaniment the rocking quaver octaves on C have become, in comparison with those in *Tel jour, telle nuit* or even in the Old Prioress's death-scene, unequivocally destructive. The nuns lower their heads, perhaps in shame for this barbarous intruder; their disorientated major triads growl in the depths of the orchestra—a breath-taking stroke of aural imagination. When the Gaoler has stomped off, the Prioress reaffirms faith by returning to the 'vow' over its ostinato bass, now a semitone higher, in E flat. At the end of the scene the main sarabande theme reappears in F sharp minor, lightened in the last three bars to the major, with a flat seventh left in suspension.

Tonality slips from F sharp to F minor again for an agitated interlude in which the Almoner reports the State's death-sentence. For the final scene we move to the Place de la Révolution, beginning with a barbaric revolutionary march, transformed into a funeral march as the nuns are lined up to face the guillotine. A minor thirds thud in the bass but the march, beginning in the Aeolian mode with chromatic alterations, proves, as the singing Carmelites march to meet death, to be a Salve Regina. The chorus ('la foule') intensify the hymn with exclamations more awed than angry, as each 'religieuse' separately mounts the scaffold, her execution being marked by a sickening thump from orchestral percussion. After the first head has fallen, the minor third ostinato shifts from A to C minor, then to G minor, as the chant gathers momentum and the orchestra weaves fragments of the sarabande-theme into the Salve Regina. Gradually, the bass too moves more freely, while the four parts acquire melodic identity, taking the place of the depleted because decapitated nuns. As heads fall more frequently, so the ostinato moves more rapidly, climaxing in a deathly dark A flat minor, which shifts to infernal F minor, and so to C minor, the key associated with the Old Prioress's death and, when minor is illuminated to a major triad with flat seventh, with transcendence.

The scalp-prickling crescendo that swells through the march-hymn grows louder as the modulations accumulate, then gradually diminishes. By the time Constance mounts the scaffold the dynamic of the C minor ostinato is soft. She smiles radiantly at Blanche as she, in fulfilment of Constance's prophecy, arrives in the nick of time to obey her vow and destiny. The moment of Constance's recognition of Blanche breaks the heart with a memory of her oscillating triads of C and A major; she meets her death singing 'O pia' on repeated Cs, over the minor triad ostinato moving from A to C as Blanche, joining her, sings 'Deo Patri fit gloria' to the familiar major third rising through a triad with flat seventh. The orchestral chords undulate from C major through D major to a dominant seventh of D flat, all over pedal C. The chord shifts back to D, but remains suspended, as the unsuspended guillotine falls. The orchestral postlude incorporates the heroic motif—C, E flat, B flat, C—that had been, at the beginning of the opera, an emblem of the Old World's grandeur (see Example 37). This makes a point, for what has been slaughtered is not only a community of nuns but also an ancestral way of life. The final tolling of bells is a requiem for a world, as well as for the souls of the decapitated nuns.

This scene never fails in emotional impact; Poulenc was justified in saying that it would make us 'weep and weep'. We weep for the defeated past; but while Poulenc leaves us in no doubt that in *Les Carmélites* the revolutionaries and the plebs are the baddies and the aristocrats and 'religieuses' are the goodies, this is not because he sees his opera as a conflict between religion and politics. *Dialogues des Carmélites* is a psychological opera before it is either religious or political, its point being that the Revolution destroyed civilized tradition, human dignity, and spiritual grace without knowing what to put in their place. Throughout his own life, which embraced two world wars, Poulenc remained dubious as to whether his beloved France had recreated those humane and spiritual values or had discovered others, but *Figure humaine* proves that he believed she needed to. He was neither a 'popular Front man' nor a die-hard conservative, but 'an old-style French Republican who once believed in liberty'.

Example 37 *Dialogues des Carmélites*: Act 2, tableau 4: p. 242 (complete but with blanks omitted).

cont.

Example 37 *cont.*

Poised between past and present, it seems probable that the impact of the last scene of *Les Carmélites* depends on Poulenc's courage in taking every possible risk. The device of the implacable crescendo and gradual diminuendo could hardly be simpler; but if one called it childish, that would pay tribute to the opera's deepest theme, since Blanche's (and Poulenc's) redemption is achieved through the agency of the child-nun Constance. What is more remarkable is that the melodrama of the beheadings—the nauseating orchestral thumps that fail to disrupt the sweep of the hymnic march—sound grotesque while at the same time enhancing the music's sublimity. This may have something to do with Poulenc's doubleness ('I am as pied as a horse'); his most bathetic depths testify to his heights. Remembering that Pierre-Octave Ferroud was beheaded in the accident that killed him in 1936, we may see the final scene of *Les Carmélites* as a desperately private horror publicly attested. Francis had a hard time deciding exactly where the thumps were to come; eventually he relied on instinct and brought it off—as only a good man, and a brave one, could have done.

Ambiguity between the sublime and the grotesque, if not the ridiculous, has another dimension in the equilibrium Poulenc sustains between world and spirit. He was 'permissive': an artist who impartially said what was to be said on behalf of God, and of the world, the flesh, and the Devil. It is not, in *Dialogues des Carmélites*, a tug-of-war between opposing forces in Blanche's psyche, paralleling those between religion and politics in the world; for Poulenc accepts these contradictions as positive values that cannot be judged in crudely relativistic terms. While the duet between Blanche and her brother sounds like passionate love-music, there is no question of a clinically incestuous relation between the siblings—Francis described their duet as being 'poised between anxiety and tenderness'. Even so, Poulenc's appetite for sensuous experience usually has sexual undertones; indeed his sexual ambivalence may condition his ambivalence between experiences sacred and profane, and this, in turn, must affect his wide appeal. He was justly proud of the musical and theatrical competence of his opera, remarking that he was ' "obnubilated" (lovely word) by my Carmelites. My familiarity with vocal music on the one hand, and the mystical ambience on the other, have enabled me to find the right tone. Obviously, people won't find it exactly amusing, but I hope and think they will be deeply moved.' His hopes were vindicated because his technical efficiency had psychological corroboration. So despite the religious subject and a predominantly female cast, the opera succeeded beyond the expectations of its commissioners at La Scala, and triumphed throughout Europe. 'Very brilliant Carmelite winter', wrote Poulenc to Bernac in 1959; 'Vienna, Naples, Palermo, Geneva, perhaps Ghent. Eleven performances this winter, fourteen planned for 1960'. If performances haven't continued at that rate, they haven't ceased, and are unlikely to; in Poulenc's opera a *figure humaine* speaks through a *voix humaine*, to which human beings respond with hearts as open as their ears.

3. *Cocteau and* La Voix humaine *(1957–1958)*

Poulenc's next and last opera was in fact called *La Voix humaine*, being a musicking, for his favourite singing actress Denise Duval, of a play by Jean Cocteau that had already achieved fame. In returning to this colleague of his youth, Francis was renewing the past in the light of the present; for the play records the woman's side of a telephone conversation between herself and a lover who had betrayed her. Poulenc confessed that he himself was vicariously this woman, with the now defunct Lucien as the paramour. Composed in 1958, the year after the *Carmélites'* première, the forty-minute, one-woman opera is thus an appendix to the major work. But whereas *Dialogues des Carmélites* had absolved personal distress in history and myth, *La Voix humaine* works in realistic and contemporary terms, exploiting techniques both high and low pertinent to French theatre. In relation to Poulenc's own amatory crisis this unabashedly secular work proves hardly less purgatorial than *Les Carmélites*.

If it seems odd that Poulenc scored so intimate a work, conceived for a quasi-speaking voice, for a large orchestra rather than for the kind of chamber ensemble he had favoured in his early theatrical pieces, the reason may be that, equating the self-sacrifice of those eighteenth-century nuns with the suicidal impulses of a sophisticated twentieth-century woman, he believed that heroic grandeur was feasible in personal terms. Indeed he knew it was, from his own experience, which paralleled that of Cocteau's fictional woman. In a letter to Aragon written in February 1959, he remarks that he 'needed the spiritual and metaphysical anguish of the Carmelites to avoid betraying the terribly human anguish of Cocteau's superb text. . . . His short phrases are so logical, so human, so charged with implications, that I have had to write a rigorously organized score, full of suspense.' To Denise Duval he admitted, in December 1959, to being 'quite overwhelmed by the recording of the work—not tearfully, but joyfully. Having brought this beautiful, sad child into the world, all that we went through for it seems worthwhile. I am now convinced that it is a masterpiece.' Poulenc may be right: for although *La Voix humaine* is not 'great' in the same sense as are *Figure humaine* and *Dialogue des Carmélites*, it triumphantly succeeds in the genre now known as 'performance art'. It is interesting that in citing 'we'—himself and Denise Duval—as makers of the opera Poulenc implies that he was doing something he had not before attempted. He also commented on the irony in the fact that these two near-autobiographical theatre works—the historical opera *Dialogues des Carmélites* and the contemporary performance-piece *La Voix humaine*—established his international reputation.

That the one-woman chamber opera, as well as the large-scale historical-mythic opera, calls for heroism is obvious in a practical sense, since one performer carries the burden of a drama which, embracing sex, love, and death, is concerned with first and last things. The woman's part is a *tour de force*, with an emotional range covering most of the qualities displayed by the complementary trio of nuns, Constance, Blanche, and the Old Prioress. The role could not be undertaken by a conventional opera singer solicitous for her 'belle voix'; only a singing actress, rather than an acting singer, could be equal to it. That Denise Duval took over as Poulenc's professional partner after Bernac, a recitalist rather than an opera singer, had retired through failing health, indicates the degree to which Poulenc was veering towards 'performance art'. At the time of his premature death he was contemplating another Cocteau opera (based on *La Machine infernale*). His last major work, *Sept Répons des ténèbres*, was a devotional act before it was concert music.

Both Cocteau and Poulenc contributed verbal prefaces to the vocal score of *La Voix humaine*. Cocteau said that the set, designed by himself to reflect at once affluence and disarray, should resemble, as he alarmingly put it, 'une chambre de meurtre'. Poulenc's notes on musical interpretation are practical. 'L'œuvre doit baigner dans la plus grande sensualité orchestrale', as an indication of a 'decadent' style of life; yet at the same time the integrity of an individual life is incarnate in the vocal line, which is often minimally accompanied and always faithful to the rhythms of the spoken word. Through this line the flesh-and-blood woman speaks, and sometimes hysterically giggles or sobs; and her immediate reality depends on her being 'une femme jeune et élégante, pas une femme âgée que son amant abandonne'. Her recitative, arioso, and occasional aria are the per-formance—the forming through—of feelings, her bodily gestures mirroring the lacerations of her heart. The orchestra too depicts, almost tactilely and visually, her physical movements as externalizations of inner distress. Its figures and motives 'auralize' things out there in the dishevelled room and even in the world beyond. Again the concept is Monteverdian: the Cocteau-Poulenc woman moves us precisely because she *is* a woman, living and breathing before our eyes and ears—as Monteverdi said of his Eurydice.

The first sounds we hear are stylizations of aural events, for a fierce trill on F sharp, accompanying an angular figure in dotted rhythm, pierces the nerves like a telephone bell awaited in dread or hope (see Example 38). This is immediately followed by two motives, the first of which, pressing up in double-dotted rhythm through a third, is identical with a basic motif—expressive of tension, aspiration, fortitude, or threat—in *Dialogues des Carmélites* (see Example 39). The second motif weeps in soft but acutely dissonant appoggiaturas. The violent disparity between these two motives prepares us for the see-saw of emotions precipitated by the clatter of the real telephone bell on stage. It isn't in fact real, for it is impersonated by a clinking xylophone: a stylization which is eerily realistic in that its metallic inhumanity punctures both

Example 38 *La Voix humaine*, p. 1, l. 1.

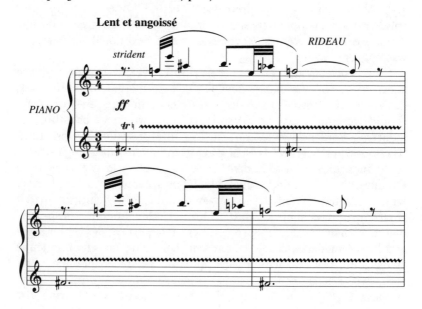

Example 39 *La Voix humaine*, p. 1, l. 3, omitting first bar.

the woman's pain and the 'sensualité' of the orchestra. In her first frantic exchanges the woman's vocal line identifies with the rhythms and pitches that would occur in real life. The orchestral barks that savage her phrases project, in their dissonance and snarling Scotch-snap rhythms, the phone's failure in communication. Since its lines are crossed, she finds herself addressing some absurd anonymous woman, instead of the man she wants. Already the opera's shifts between 'l'angoisse' and 'le calme' are manifest: not for nothing does Poulenc say in his preface that the interpretation must be in the hands of the singer, assisted, *where necessary*, by the conductor.

After the woman has angrily replaced the receiver, the double-dotted, upward-thrusting figure recurs more fiercely; we may hear in it her muttered curses. The xylophone-telephone clatters again, administering its physical and nervous shock. This time she is through to the man, conversing in nervous speech-rhythms and semi-pitches. We gather, as she talks, that her lover is trying to make their separation definitive, though she interprets his remarks in pitiful hopefulness. We in the audience cannot of course hear what he says; but Cocteau's subtle text leaves no doubt as to their 'dualistic' tensions. She spins webs of fancy, kidding herself but never the lover. She pretends she is surviving, getting on with a 'normal' life; describes what she is dressed in (but isn't); reminds him of special moments in their relationship. She even shamingly claims that the breakdown has been all her fault; but balks at his demand that she should return their love-letters.

At the first reference to the letters a single chromatic strand accompanies the voice, followed by more expansive chords to which she abases herself. But the human spirit is resilient: from self-abasement springs her first lyrical efflorescence, as she nostalgically recalls some 'dimanche de Versailles', in a phrase richly harmonized in the C sharp minor that had had such erotic charge in *Dialogues des Carmélites*, as well as in many of Poulenc's finest love-songs. Both melody and harmony are Ravelian, though the fragmentation may indicate that the man's memories are less fond than hers. As the one-sided dialogue stumbles on, shifts in tempo and mood reflect now agony, now hope, now assumed indifference; the orchestra contributes to the conversation, toying with an angular figure recalling the opening bars of the opera, and emulating the telephone's inhumane, along with the woman's humane but grief-contorted, voice. Lyric drama evolves through, not in spite of, fragmentariness; indeed, the non-progression of the orchestral motives is the point; that they 'get nowhere' is the essence of the, or at least of this, human predicament.

In the midst of her prevarications the woman is again 'cut off', her exasperation audible in barking rhythms and snarling dissonances. Exhausted, she replaces the receiver to a 'très calme' sequence of chromatic chords, again punctured by the xylophone-telephone. But it isn't the man, only his man-servant: she learns that her ex-lover is not at home. The woman's conversation with the servant is fairly calm—she must find it a relief to talk to a relatively disinterested person. But no sooner has she replaced the receiver than a molto agitato return of the rising third motif heralds another blast from the telephone. This time it is the lover, and the panic of the woman's response is underlined by the nagging, Scotch-snapped rhythms—at once physical gestures and stifled sobs. Lushly lovely chromatics accompany her 'très sensuel et lyrique' admission that she had lied to him in pretending that she was getting on with her life, whereas in fact 'je devenais folle',

Example 40 *La Voix humaine*, p. 34, l. 3.

on a high C at that (see Example 40). Over an obsessive ostinato
she swears ('tendrement enfantine') to do anything he asks of her,
and croons an arioso in slow 9/8, 'douloureux mais très simple'.
Poulenc compared this to Sibelius's *Valse triste*, and that that
insidious piece had become a corny Palm Court number points to
the element of self-deception not only in her lies, but also in her
forlorn attempts to tell the truth.

For in the course of the waltz she confesses to having
attempted suicide by way of her sleeping pills: the havering of the
tonality between tragic C minor and bland A flat major enhances
ambivalence, since she is simultaneously trying emotionally to
'come clean' and to cosset her pain in a dream. She admits that
'je n'avais pas le courage de mourir seule'; and irresolutely swaying chords—dominant seventh of E flat in second inversion, followed by E minor with added seventh—accompany her sobs on
the word 'chéri'. She drugs herself on her pendulum-swaying
rhythms and on Ravelian chromatics as she imagines the two of
them curled up in bed. We don't know what the lover does during her long *valse*-arioso and her 'très calme et voluptueux' day-
dream; perhaps he snatches a nap himself, or toys with a
crossword puzzle. At this stage we can't help feeling a certain
sympathy for him, or at least impatience with the woman comparable with that which Bernac felt with Poulenc in the wilderness
of his despair over Lucien (see Bernac's letter, quoted on
p. 180). Poulenc's courage, in unflinchingly recording his and the

woman's indignity, earns our grudging respect. In the context of the opera, however, the man is given a moment's respite because the woman is enraged by loud ragtimey music in the next flat. Under this external assault she collapses; and there is a 'très long' silence, out of which the woman admits, to forlorn parallel thirds in false relation, that 'c'est inutile'. The doctor will call again tomorrow but, 'au comble de la lassitude', she sighs to drooping dominant sevenths on E and C, three times repeated.

Her deflation is perhaps in part a ruse, for although 'hagarde', she pulls herself together with the aid of an orchestral monody expanded from the familiar double-dotted figure. In a 'très lyrique' episode she abjectly apologizes for having irritated her one-time lover—even as the orchestra flowers into a full-blown tune similar to, and even more opulent than, her love-reminiscence in C sharp minor. Poulenc is hardly a Blakean figure, but he does approach a 'terrifying honesty' in here admitting to self-deceit: for the music suggests not so much Ravel as Puccini, than whom no composer has more powerfully revealed the truth latent within cliché. Puccini was the quintessential media composer before the mass media were invented. Poulenc's Pucciniesque moment does not have the high voltage of the master himself, nor would that be in tune with Francis or his heroine. The point is rather that the woman's extravagant emotion, like that of Poulenc in the trauma over Lucien, must seem, in the context of a pretend-apology, sentimental because in excess of the object; and it is certainly phoney in a punning sense, since she plays with the telephone chord, now the sole, pathetically mechanical, dismally inefficient, preserver of their one-time togetherness. All afflatus dissipated, she croons to her rocking chords and syncopated bass of how she does nothing except lie in bed, clutching the telephone, willing it to ring, terrified lest it might. The meaningless inconsequence of minutes, hours, and days is interrupted by what might be a synonym for it, a snatch of the trivial rag-music from next door, which shatters her reverie. She launches into an anecdote about her little dog—an attempt to displace the self into something or someone outside it. The attempt is unsuccessful because the little dog, who seems to be failing, probably dying, *is* herself, and she knows it.

During this self-communing a single, frail chromatic line and Satiean unrelated concords float wistfully through the recitative, which is shattered when the anonymous woman on the crossed line intervenes. This is the last turn of the screw or twist of the knife: for although the woman succeeds, abetted by gruff orchestral barks and dotted-rhythmed rising thirds and falling tritones, in banishing the intruder, it is not clear whether the woman re-establishes contact with the man, or merely chatters to his ghost. She sing-speaks of his extreme benignity, in contrast with that wicked woman who keeps sundering their communion; she finds it better to identify a source of evil 'out there' than to admit that it may be within herself. Her plight is again aurally imaged in that oscillation of a dominant seventh of E flat with an F minor triad with flat seventh—a device that has obvious affinities with Blanche's tonal ambiguities in *Les Carmélites*.

Singing more to herself than her lover (who may not be there), she meditates on the unpredictability of love and hate and of the ultimate failure of human communication. The music's delicious melancholy belies her thought or feeling that 'le mieux est de faire comme moi et de s'en moquer complètement'; and we are unsure how far her capitulation to fate is a self-indulgent game, and how far it is a genuine act of acceptance. For she yearns, with a recurrence of the dotted rhythm and the ostinato of swaying chords, for a contact more real than can accrue from this inimical machine, yet lulls herself again with her 9/8 *valse triste*, murmuring that no one commits suicide twice, albeit regretting that 'j'aurais du avoir du courage'. The *valse* merges into her wavering chords in triple time; and the passage is shifted up a tone, and then a semitone, as she murmurs of illusion and reality, of lies and truth, hardly knowing or even caring which is which. She is cut off again; and admits that, knowing he lied to her, she could love him with 'plus de tendresses'. Apparently, this exactly reflects the end of Poulenc's affair with Lucien.

The final episode opens 'très calme et morne', to an ostinato of quavers and repeated notes not dissimilar to the music for the incarcerated Carmelites, just before their execution. To these winding strands of melody the woman slowly winds the telephone chord around her throat. Her recitative is related to the lyricism of her C sharp minor love-song, supported by those calm but falsely related Satiean concords (see Example 41). A return of the dominant seventh of E flat, swaying to an E minor triad, summons her lover's ghost; she begs him, since he is going to Marseilles tomorrow, not to stay in the little hotel sacred to them. Inevitably, the love-song floats in the orchestra, though she cannot

Example 41 *La Voix humaine*, p. 66, l. 3.

au comble de la tendresse

J'ai ta voix au-tour de mon cou.___ Ta voix au-

tour de mon cou.___

sing it herself, and it is in neutral A minor rather than charismatic C sharp minor. The motto-chords sound again at the original pitch, but subside downwards as she hopes that, if she cut off consciousness like a telephone line, 'les choses que j'imagine pas n'existent pas'. She ends with a thank you, presumably to the man for having once existed, and with the confession 'Je t'aime'.

She lies on the bed, to the ostinato of repeated quavers and oscillating thirds, beginning on love's C sharp but declining chromatically to end on A minor, the basic tonality of *La Voix humaine*, as it had been of *Dialogues des Carmélites*. A rising cantilena swells on the orchestra over a tonic pedal and rocking quavers. The melody, flowering from the double-dotted figures, resembles the nobly pathetic theme of the Agnus of the *Gloria* that Poulenc had recently completed: so that it would seem that, notwithstanding her (and Poulenc's) neurasthenic self-abasement, she does effect a sacrificial act comparable, in private rather than public terms, with the nuns' communal relinquishment. The woman learns courage to face death rather than submit to shame and self-betrayal—as well as betrayal by a Lucien-like lover. Ultimately, this grand theme elicits grandly tragic music, less sustained than the closing scene of *Les Carmélites*, though dominated by the same implacably falling A minor thirds. The intimate affinities between the woman's music and that of Blanche are evidence of Poulenc's identification of his private with his public theme.

Cocteau's device of the telephone conversation as a synonym for the alienation inherent in modern life—the too easy access of one human creature to another, and the still easier severance of the one from the other—is adapted by Poulenc with just the right balance between realism and stylization. Seismographically recording the vagaries of both the subconscious and the conscious (or at least the half-conscious) mind, he creates momentum, if not growth and development, from a succession of moments. His momentariness—which connects him to 'performance art'—is his modernity: which may be why *La Voix humaine* rivets the attention throughout its forty-minute span. Another reason for Poulenc's abiding popularity would seem to be that he stands as scapegoat for us all. He needed his full symphony orchestra not merely to evoke a luxurious and possibly effete society, but still more to be morally equal to its relinquishment. The 'mœurs' implicit in *La Voix humaine* are very different from those implicit in *Dialogues des Carmélites*; but the agony and the courage of their relinquishment are the same.

7
POULENC ENTRE L'ÉGLISE ET LA SALLE DE CONCERT

1. Quatre Petites Prières de Saint François d'Assise *(1948) and* Quatre Motets pour le temps de Noël *(1952)*

The religious music of Poulenc's Rocamadour years had consequences a decade or two later. After the Second World War he sought relaxation from the war's turmoil and from the intensity of this music in letting off steam in his Apollinaire-based *opéra bouffe, Les Mamelles de Tirésias*; he also wrote, in 1948, a religious work that fulfils a comparable function, for the *Quatre Petites Prières de Saint François d'Assise* take their texts from a saint famous for benevolence towards created nature. Moreover, these prayers are liturgical in a basic sense, since they were written for the male voices of the brothers of Champfleury Monastery, and were dedicated 'à Frère Jérôme en souvenir de son grandpère: mon oncle, Camille Poulenc'. The link between familial interests and a religious community is to the point, for monkish life and music had proved therapeutic during Francis's religious crisis and nervous distress.

The first prayer is an initially simple hymn to the Virgin, with the tenors singing a Renaissance-style melody beginning with rising fifths, while baritones sustain a bagpipe-like drone, 'bouche fermée'. But the second clause transmutes E flat major into minor, which is undermined by enharmonic identification of E flat with D sharp. Further enharmonies further uproot us: but carry us back to E flat as we appeal for the Virgin's compassion, 'infidèles' though we be. The melodic line, however, is chromaticized, and even the bagpipe drone wobbles a little. The final cadence compromises: approached by one of Poulenc's favourite dominant sevenths, it resolves on to God's perfect fifth, eschewing the warmth of the third.

The second prayer is monkish incantation addressed to 'le souverain Dieu'. The texture, 'majestueux et éclatant', is homophonic, at speech rhythm, basically in D flat. In the middle section enharmonies imbue praise with awe; and the sudden return to D flat major stops the breath, as the final cadence sidles from a D minor triad to a major triad of D flat. The third prayer equates love of God with death, in which we hope to find him. In heavenly E major, it begins syllabically, 'très expressif et fervent', garnering chromatics as 'je meure par amour de votre amour'. Again the cadence on to the major triad is magic (see Example 42). In the final prayer solo tenor fulfils a priestly function in leading the company from stepwise-moving monody into homophony wherein human suffering is juxtaposed with the infinity of God's glory. Pedal notes on G support the flowing can-tillation, which embraces dissonant chromatics at the forbidding news that whereas 'beaucoup sont appelés, peu sont élus'. The final cadence resolves a variously modal G minor into benign G major; Poulenc's faith, which he himself called naïve, had some-thing in common with the saint of Assisi.

Example 42   *Quatre Petites Prières*, no. 3, p. 8, last three bars.

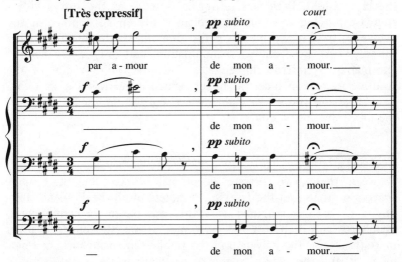

A few years later, in 1952, Poulenc wrote a set of a cappella motets for mixed voices, which he intended to be life-giving natal music to balance the penitential motets of 1938–9. The *Quatre Motets pour le temps de Noël* resemble the penitential motets in deriving their idiom from French Renaissance music although, given the subject, they are slighter than the earlier set. They are not, however, less magical—as is immediately audible in the first motet, 'O magnum mysterium', which takes its text from the fifth response for matins on Christmas Day. The mystery of mysteries is the birth of a saviour among the humble beasts of the byre, and Poulenc finds an apt musical image for this light shining in darkness: the three lower parts hover between a dark B flat minor triad and what sounds like a triad of G major, though its B natural is notated as C flat. Above this, trebles float tenderly down a fourth from high F, a phrase which intermittently returns, dropping like balm, always *ppp*. In the middle section the music moves sharpwards over a G bass, reaching, at the reference to 'Dominum Christum', the many-sharped region of B major. An enharmonic change of A sharp to B flat proves a pivot on which the original B flat minor is re-established, with the trebles' refrain on top. The final cadence, a *tierce de Picardie* to B flat *major*, is a blessed consummation.

'Quem vidistis pastores dicite' tells the old tale of the 'sely shepherds' who are afforded a glimpse of angels flitting around the Holy Child. Poulenc's setting is as naïve as the story, with a stepwise moving tune in the Aeolian mode on B, doubled at the octave by trebles and tenors, while altos hum a descant in parallel thirds. There is virtually no modulation, and only a few fleeting chromatics to mirror the angelic concourse. The vision of the Annunciation is in lucent B major, which is again not a shift to a new base; and the motet ends with a slightly enriched da capo of the first tune and words.

2. Stabat Mater *for Soli, chorus, and Orchestra (1950)*

Between these two private devotional works—the St Francis prayers of 1948 and the Christmas motets of 1952—Poulenc composed, in 1950, a religious work that was public in being scored for chorus and orchestra and performed at the Strasbourg Festival in 1951. Again, the private and the public dimensions are complementary; and the public aspects of the work had a private spur to their inception. Poulenc had considered writing a requiem for his painter-friend Christian Bérard, but abandoned the ideas as being too portentous. The more intimate medieval text of the *Stabat Mater*, portraying the anguish of the Mother of God at the foot of the Cross, seemed more appropriate to Francis's temperament, and had the technical advantage that the text, being sectionally stanzaic, could be presented quasi-liturgically, without developed structure, symphonic or operatic. Because the text offers 'flashes' between the physical agony of the Son on the Cross and the spiritual torment of the Mother standing at his feet, Poulenc had no need to apologize for episodic technique. Considerable stretches of the *Stabat Mater* are a cappella, like short motets. The orchestra is used to point crucial moments in the crucial story, but formally the work functions in a region between liturgical commentary and a structure organized in musical terms. This accords with Poulenc's struggle, during the 1950s, to shape up to the large-scale forms his 'grand' opera, *Dialogues des Carmélites*, would necessitate. The *Stabat Mater* came to be regarded by Poulenc as a study for *Les Carmélites*, both works being related to the love/death of Lucien Roubert. Poulenc confessed that the grandly grim purgatorial motives in both works had been inspired by Stravinsky's *Oedipus Rex*, which he justifiably regarded as a supreme masterpiece of the twentieth century. (See his magniloquent letter to Stravinsky, dated 30 May 1927.)

The first movement of the *Stabat Mater* gives no intimation of the work's kaleidoscopic technique, for it is a noble piece on a large scale, beginning in a slow four-pulse over a tonic pedal of A minor, with a swinging accompaniment of quavers in thirds and sixths, grouped in pairs. When the choric basses invoke the Mother standing dolorously at the Cross, they sing pentatonic minor thirds, anticipatory of those pervasive in *Dialogues des Carmélites*, centred on the same Aeolian A minor. As the voices accumulate, the paragraphs are spacious, the sobriety of the unbroken rhythm serving to discipline the volatile modulations. At the reference to the Son on his Cross the thirds rock, as might be expected, in F minor, while trombones add bite to the leaping sixth and plunging diminished seventh in the bass. Most of the music is repeated to the same words, winding its way back through a German sixth to A minor. Unaccompanied chorus chants the final word 'filius' on a sustained A minor triad. Seldom has a minor triad sounded so irremediably minor.

'Cujus aninam gementes' preserves the minor thirds but hoists them up a semitone to B flat minor, throbbing in a quick, syncopated 3/8. Flickering demisemiquavers are serpentine, perhaps prompted by the words 'pertranssivit gladius'; pedal notes in the bass suggest thumping hearts; tonality quivers from B flat to C minor, but ends in 'lugubrious' F minor. Whereas this stanza concerns the Son's physical torment, the next is about the Mother's mental pain. 'O quam tristis' is extremely slow, and a cappella in B minor, subsiding to E flat minor. The benediction of Mary lilts between A flat minor and a dominant seventh of C, but with C sharp as bass (see Example 43). A da capo of a cappella music fades in an orchestral postlude on a long-sustained B minor triad.

Example 43 *Stabat Mater*, p. 16, l. 1, last four bars (voices only).

The painful fervour of this stanza contrasts oddly with the next, which tells us that 'Christ above in torment hangs while she beneath beholds his pangs.' That the verse, certainly in English and to a degree in the original Latin, is doggerel perhaps encouraged Poulenc to set it to cheerily flowing music in bland A flat major, thereby distinguishing Mary's vicarious experience from her Son's real right thing. There is no change in the regular quaver pulse, and only straightforward modulations to C and F. The occasional chromatics sound more graceful, even witty, than anguished. The penultimate chord is a second inversion of A flat, with added *major* seventh instead of Poulenc's habitual blue seventh.

This curious stanza prepares us for the 'Quis est homo', which twists dulcet A flat major into the original A minor; semitonic key-shifts in this work frequently underline emotional contradiction. Here tempo is frenetic, repeated semiquavers being punctured by savage brass. Minor thirds are highlighted by trombones and explode in a prestissimo whirligig of triplets on the words 'pro peccatis suae gentis', in C sharp or D flat, major or minor. The final seven bars furiously assert a dominant-tonic cadence in B flat minor, which again makes a paradoxical preparation for the 'Vidit suum', once more yanked up a semitone to B minor, with a nobly singing cello and bass line supporting pulsing B minor triads. Soprano solo chants a magnificent phrase falling from high F sharp to the B below middle C, pervaded by the double-dotted rhythm that in Poulenc, as in many classical composers, may signify physical pain (see Example 44). In the coda the soprano soloist repeats this phrase, beginning, in tragic majesty, a tone higher on G sharp. Ultimately she cries 'Dum emisit' to a rising and falling B minor triad, while the orchestra supports her with tonic pedal notes and floating thirds and sixths, as in the preludial movement, only a tone higher.

Example 44   *Stabat Mater*, p. 30, ll. 1 and 2 (soprano solo only).

Typically, this high point is followed by a low in the form of a child-like address to the Mother, in fast 3/8 and in straight E flat major, the texture smiling in parallel thirds. When we ask to be 'irradiated' by Mary's love and Christ's pain there is a nerviness in the palpitating rhythm, but modulations in the middle never threaten disruption, and the da capo of the parallel thirds affords delight, even if the final cadence contains a slight shiver. In the next stanza danger is past, as we appeal to Mary to help us to 'glow and melt', as did she, with love of Christ. The stanza begins severely, with a (for Poulenc) unusual approach to a fugal texture in grave C sharp minor. But when the orchestra joins the a cappella texture, it wafts in parallel dominant sevenths: a Debussyan moment—perhaps prompted by the word 'complaceam'—such as is rare in Poulenc.

The 'Sancta Mater' asks that we may share in Mary's grief, if not in her son's pain. A declamatory introduction compromises between B flat and C minor, and the main allegretto is mysterious and contrarious, as though we are scared, as well we might be, of the prospect before us. For the 'Virgo virginium praeclara', radiant F sharp major becomes a fundament, with chromatic scales thrusting through middle register, gradually dying away. A final a cappella setting of the words 'Fac me tecum plangere' modulates from F sharp minor to B minor, only to conclude orchestrally with three chords of B flat minor. We do not know *where* we are, but find out in the finely sustained setting of 'Fac ut portem Christi mortem' which, with yet another semitonic shift, is in A minor. This music, in sarabande rhythm and with heroic double dots, anticipates the opening of the last act of *Dialogues des Carmélites* and is scarcely less moving. Again, the end is calm, on a C sharp major triad with blue flat seventh.

'Inflammatus et accensus' reanimates the medieval poet's latent terror. Fearing lest he and we may be consumed not in the flames of divine love but in those of Judgment Day, he prays for the Mother's succour. The movement divides into two brief sections, the first fear-stricken in B minor, with throbbing pedal notes and alternating minor thirds, the second a cappella and slow, once more a semitone apart in B flat minor, subsiding to E flat minor when the male voices are haloed by swaying chords over a dominant pedal. The protracted cadence on 'Ad palman victoriae' leads into the last stanza 'Quando corpus morietur', still in E flat minor, in slow-swaying triple pulse. After alternating but falsely related concords the soloist, floating from the choral and orchestral sonority, gloriously unfurls the 'Paradisi gloria' in E flat major. But the choral and orchestral music gravitates, a cappella, to remote A minor, a devilish tritone away from E flat. In bars of alternating A minor and major the soloist wafts on high a radiantly pentatonic version of the chant (see Example 45).

We have noted that the technique of Poulenc's *Stabat Mater*, like that of the medieval poem, is episodic, and that one of the consequences of this is the frequency with which the stanzas are shifted a semitone or a tone away from one another. Poulenc

144

Example 45 *Stabat Mater*, p. 66, l. 1, omitting first bar (voices only).

counteracts this kaleidoscopic approach by the cross-references he makes between movements, and by his large-scale handling of tonality. Thus the ultimate 'Paradisi gloria' is set to a quasi-liturgical incantation of repeated notes and falling thirds, while the orchestra refers to the first movement's paired quavers. Circuitously, tonality seeks and again finds E flat minor, while the chorus continues its incantation in dotted rhythms and repeated notes. Suddenly, the choral Amen is loudly sonorous in E flat major, but ends on a dissonance, which the orchestra caps with an immense chord of E flat minor with added flat seventh. The triple forte dynamic and the harsh scoring discourage us from taking this as Poulenc's typical suspension of Time; it sounds more like an assertion of willed faith in timelessness, the wilfulness perhaps being a consequence of the composer's current psychological trauma. If E flat major is in this work the key of Glory, its end in E flat minor is a compromise with subconscious allegorical undertones. Six-flatted E flat minor is traditionally a deathly key but, being the minor of the *Stabat*'s key of glory, is closer to transcendence than is the work's earthily basic A minor (a tritone apart). In context, the effect of this E flat minor close is slightly odd: startling when one doesn't expect, or want, to be startled. Even so, Poulenc came through. Within a year he was working on *Dialogues des Carmélites*, which cost him dear but (as we have noted) earned him salvation. Immediately, the opera was followed by a *Gloria*, in which the glorious key is not E flat, but traditionally benedictory G major.

3. Gloria *for Soprano Solo, Chorus, and Orchestra (1959)*

The origins of Poulenc's *Gloria* were not unconnected with the triumph of *Dialogues des Carmélites*, for that in part prompted the Koussevitsky Foundation to offer Poulenc a commission for a major work in memory of the two Koussevitskys, recently deceased. The Foundation asked for a symphony, the respect-worthy form for a prestigious assignment, but Poulenc declined on the grounds that he was no symphonist. The Foundation's second choice was an organ concerto: to which Francis retorted that he had already written one, and didn't fancy another. When the commissioners capitulated to the extent of accepting anything the composer favoured, he came up with a *Gloria* for soprano solo, chorus, and orchestra. He thought of it not only as a tribute to the Koussevitskys, but as paying a debt of gratitude to God, with whose help Francis had laid the ghost of Lucien and had completed, in *Dialogues des Carmélites*, his most ambitious creation—which had, moreover, been blest with international success. Poulenc composed the *Gloria* between May and December in 1959. He had celebrated his sixtieth birthday on 7 January.

'When I wrote this piece', said Poulenc, 'I had in mind those frescoes by Gozzoli where the angels stick out their tongues. And also some serious Benedictine monks I had once seen revelling in a game of football.' So Janus-Poulenc reconciles the opposites, fusing his roles as 'enfant terrible', as 'dévot', and as 'bonhomme' in one work which is symphonic in concept, and more highly organized than the collage-styled *Stabat Mater*. Significantly, he composed this potently positive piece with great care, remarking apropos of it:

Often, during my fits of self-doubt, I ask myself if it is not sterility that causes me to compose so slowly. But since I have chosen this path, I must stick to it. I cannot, like Milhaud, play ducks and drakes with my talent. One day I will explain to you exactly how I have constructed this *Gloria*. Anyway, I think the sound quality of the end will be very beautiful. I love the voice so much.

If the *Gloria* pays off a debt to God, it is appropriate that it should be a summation of the various, often contradictory, strands from which Poulenc's music had been woven. The instrumental introduction, dominated by brass fanfares, harks back to *Les Biches*, for its majestic gait and double-dotted rhythms recall the France of Louis XIV, for Poulenc an ideal, if unreal, civilization. That this dream-world is impermanent becomes patent in the closing bars of the prelude, for the brazen sonorities dissipate and tonality changes from joyous G major to tragic G minor, the music now scored for woodwinds in parallel fourths and sevenths. Clouds are dispersed as the chorus enters, singing Glorias in double-dotted rhythms, through surging parallel thirds in the orchestra, over a bass pounding between minor thirds of B minor. Although both the key and the minor thirds could imply tragic issues, here they relate rather to the ritualism of *Les Biches*; and grow increasingly exuberant even when, or perhaps because, the music modulates into such dark keys as E flat, B flat, and F minors. At the reference to men of good will (whom God may bless) the music wings lyrically through declining sequences, returning by way of

B flat major to G major, with the oscillating thirds in the bass. The brass fanfares of the opening reappear, and the movement closes in paeans of glory, with pulsing semiquavers forming B minor triads over a pedal G as bass. This synthesis of 'blessed' G major with 'suffering' B minor will recur, and is the clue to the work's sublime end.

A hint of Stravinsky's neo-Russian primitivism, latent in the first movement, becomes patent in 'Laudamus te', which is 'très vif et joyeaux', and for a considerable time in 'white' C major. The music differs from Stravinsky in being 'enfantine' in manner, with short phrases bandied between the voices, often over oompah basses; the 60-year-old composer's glorification is as youthful as the wedding music in *Les Biches*. When modulations occur, they move in neat sequences that soon bounce back to white C major, and to a reminiscence of the telescoped diatonic triads of the first movement. After an 'altered' subdominant chord and a long silence, Poulenc offers one of his glimpses 'over the rainbow': altos sing 'Gratias agimus' in a chromaticized mode, floating in mysterious string chords. This intimation of mortality, and perhaps of immortality, recalls *Les Biches*'s never-never land; as does the resumed allegro, initially in E flat, perky over the oompah bass. The concluding lauds are back in white C major, glitteringly scored. Since tonics, dominants, and subdominants resound simultaneously, time is liquidated in primitive fiesta, an effect enhanced by the deliberately perverse accentuation. Poulenc must have picked this up from Stravinsky's handling of Latin texts, though whereas the effect in the Russian's music is ritualistically hieratic, in Poulenc's music it is juvenilely naïve.

Yet Poulenc's *Gloria* is far from being a reversion to childhood; the next section, turning from us celebrating mortals to the Lord God (Domine Deus) testifies to Poulenc not only as 'dévot', but also as grown up. The triple tempo is 'très lent et calme', the key is 'suffering' B minor, and the words are sung by solo soprano to a noble phrase based on a falling fifth, soon capped with a wondrous flowering on the words 'Pater omnipotens', with solo horn in canon with the voice (see Example 46). A middle section occurs as the tempo changes from 3/4 to 4/4; ripe modulations are resolved by way of a 'Neapolitan' C major, serving as transition to a B major *tierce de Picardie*. Characteristically, solo horn adds a flat seventh, suspended in time and space, to the final triad.

After this near-sublime presentation of the Godhead, Poulenc

Example 46 *Gloria*, p. 22, l. 2, bars 2 and 3.

again depicts us worshippers as God's children. 'Domine fili uni-
genite' is back in G major, and is as ludically 'vite et joyeux' as
the most unbuttoned moments in *Les Biches*. The lines prance in
scales and arpeggios, plain diatonic with sidekicks to grammati-
cally unrelated keys; the vocal parts are often pentatonic. Regular
recurrences of the rondo tune mean that our feet, however frisky,
don't entirely leave the ground; even in the final section, when the
music modulates, flatwards, the manner is still playful. Perhaps
this is the bit inspired by the footballing Benedictines; in any case
this fleet-footed scherzo serves as foil to the climactic movement,
celebrating both Domine Deus and his human Lamb-Son.

After two introductory bars, the first in savage false relations,
the orchestra swings in a slow aria scored for woodwind, with a
pendulum-like accompaniment, sometimes harshly scored, in B
flat minor. There is a high baroque flourish in the woodwind
skirls that precede the soprano solo, whose opening phrase
embraces both an augmented fourth and an augmented fifth (see
Example 47). As the chorus dialogues with the soloist, her phrase
is modified until it gives birth to a new theme whose stable
repeated crotchets affirm certainties in a sinful world. Climax
comes when the theme originally in B flat minor returns a tone

Example 47 *Gloria*, p. 35, l. 2, bar 2 (soprano solo).

lower, in sepulchral A flat minor. The soprano solo again proves a saviour, for her 'Qui tollis' phrase steers us back, by way of E flat, to the wide-flung tritonal theme in B flat minor. She chants her final 'Qui tollis' in Mixolydian F major, the textures divided between woodwind, strings, and horns. The movement ends with a triple-piano triad of E flat minor—a fifth lower than the basic B flat. The effect is at once depressive and resolutory.

From the final setting of 'Qui sedes ad dexteram Patrem' the sacrificial lamb is at first banished. The chorus intones the words in unison, in the work's original G major, interspersed with brazen blasts from the orchestra, quoting both the double-dotted melodic figure and the simultaneous G major-B minor triads of the first movement. The main setting of 'Qui sedes' is in fast 4/4, with a walking bass in quavers and running semiquavers in the inner parts. The babble of G major is often assaulted by orchestral eruptions of the double-dotted figure. The padding quavers and tripping semiquavers cavort through many keys, periodically called to order by the brass fanfares, which grow more urgent and more frequent to counteract the spate.

The justly famous final section recapitulates the words of the 'Qui sedes' while the orchestra, 'extraordinairement calme', weaves a texture of G major and B minor arpeggios, over a pedal G. Comparisons with the end of Stravinsky's *Symphony of Psalms* are often made, though the serene modality of the vocal lines and the radiance of the harmony are closer to Ravel. But the idiom remains essential Poulenc, and the last 'misereres' reaffirm the parallel sevenths and ninths of the first movement with a grandeur that banishes self-pity, though we are admitting that the pity of God would not come amiss. The chorus chants the first movement's simultaneous chords of B minor and G major, while the orchestra blazes in double-dotted fanfares. The ultimate choral-orchestral chords are triple-piano fusions of G major and B minor, through which the soloist floats an Amen on D, fifth of G major and third of B minor. This epilogic spelling-out of the interdependence of 'blessed' G major and 'tragic' B minor may be fortuitous but is none the less potent. The 'lost' state of the *Stabat Mater* and the purgatorial agony of *Dialogues des Carmélites* meet in a hearteningly positive work that is never evasive. Not for nothing has the *Gloria* become the most popular of Poulenc's larger works, with an established place in the repertory.

4. Laudes de Saint Antoine de Padoue *for Male Voices (1959) and* Sept Répons des ténèbres *for Treble Solo, Chorus, and Orchestra (1960–1961)*

Poulenc's final religious works were not, however, concert pieces but liturgical acts, even though the larger of them was commissioned by the New York Philharmonic. The small work preludial to the big one was the *Laudes de Saint Antoine de Padoue*, written for male voices in 1959. Unlike the St Francis prayers, the piece does not seem to have been associated with a religious community, though it is certainly music of liturgical *action*. St Anthony, most celebrated among St Francis's acolytes, was Poulenc's favourite saint, perhaps because of his practicality as a worker of miracles and reputed recoverer of lost property. Poulenc sets his prayers in the original Latin, in a style so direct that we seem to be in the presence of men praising their maker in melodies that have the fervour of monkish cantillation, along with the raw virility of Italian folk-song. These monks are simultaneously children of God and agrarian peasants: so the work fulfils Poulenc's hope that his faith might be 'that of a country priest', and reminds us that his cult of childhood was in no sense escapist. Though children may be 'innocent', they are none the less creatures of the Fall, and may be wicked without knowing they are.

The first praise-song, a hymn to Jesus, though marked 'très calmement', begins double forte: its tranquility is that of faith and fortitude, rather than of spiritual serenity. The initial monody for baritone is Aeolian, stepwise-moving, spacious; when the three parts move together, each is independently declamatory, in clearly defined patterns, even when an occasional chromatic intrudes. Bare fourths and fifths lend austerity; wide leaps, especially in the bass part, inculcate energy without the progressive implications of 'Western' harmony. The laud ends, in St-Anthony-like practicality, with an appeal to Jesus to kindle fire in his servants, so that they may perform both their religious and their domestic duties more efficaciously. The three parts are at first exclamatory, but on the repetitions of the word 'donet' high tenors and low basses rock in octaves, while second tenors and basses undulate in chromatized organum, left suspended on an A major triad with blue flat seventh. This is a positive manifestation of the blue notes common in Poulenc's early music, telling us that there can be no end (and no full cadence) to the worship of God for the obvious reason that he is beyond Time.

The second laud, 'O Proles', is addressed to St Anthony himself, scourge of the faithless and bringer of light. Until the penultimate bar the piece is in three parts, tenor, baritone, bass: one of which intones the saint's name is repeated quavers on G, 'comme une psalmodie', while another part boldly declaims the text. The mode is Dorian on G, and the vigorous lines sound earthy rather than ecclesiastical. Hypnotic repetitions suggest primitive ritual, reminiscent of Stravinsky's *Les Noces*. In the last two bars, on the word 'inane', the bass falls through an octave while the upper parts are divided, to cease on a fortissimo chord involving a blue thirteenth as well as seventh!

'Laus regi', though again marked 'très calmement', begins in fortissimo tenor monody in the Dorian mode on E. An answering clause in two parts remains sturdily modal, presenting Anthony as a stern soldier of Christ; but at the reference to 'Antoni, vir egregie' the texture divides softly into four parts, undulating in unrelated triads (see Example 48). The sequence of loud monodic incantation followed by soft chromatically wavering triads is repeated, as though to insist on the distinction between the atemporal certitudes of God and the temporal fallibilities of a mere man, however saintly. There is a mystery in this that makes the piece religious in a more basic, though not more moving, sense than the personally expressive *Motets de pénitence*. The hymn Amens on a chord of celestial E major, but in second inversion and with flat seventh. Although the words tell us that we are washed clean of sin, the unresolved final chord appends a question mark.

The fourth and last laud celebrates, at marching pace, St Anthony's powers as a miracle-worker. The mode havers between Aeolian and Dorian on D, the lines alternating between stepwise movement and wide leaps. When the words claim that through the saint's offices danger may be dispelled, the music paradoxically reflects, in vacillating chromatics, the peril and perturbation, while only the bass, rocking through fourths and fifths, promotes stability. In the coda these godly intervals win the day, resonating in the tenors while the basses plunge in octave unisons. Once more the amen is a second inversion of a dominant seventh, this time on D. Though it still ends on a question mark this laud is devotional action-music more direct in impact than anything in Poulenc's previous work.

Example 48   *Laudes de Saint Antoine*: 'Laus regi', p. 11, last two lines.

These laudes might be considered as a study for Poulenc's last, and perhaps most remarkable, devotional piece, the *Sept Répons des ténèbres* for treble solo, chorus, and orchestra, on which he embarked in the following year, 1960. Poulenc approached the sacred texts for Holy Week—some of which he had drawn on for his penitential motets, more than twenty years previously—in Kirkegaardian fear and trembling, even though, or perhaps the more because, the work had been commissioned by Leonard Bernstein and the New York Philharmonic, for the prestigious opening of the Lincoln Centre, New York, in 1962. Francis's choice of texts may have reflected intimations of mortality at the close of his own life: for although the heart attack that killed him at the early age of 63 was unexpected, he had been variously ailing; physical malfunctionings had accompanied his nervous prostration during the affair of Lucien. There is characteristic courage in Poulenc's creating so tenebrously religious a work for the grandiose gala of a state opening. He made no attempt to camouflage its nature, for he not only chose traditional liturgical texts, but also insisted on boy choristers for the vocal parts, however streamlined the orchestra.

The first *répons*, for Holy Thursday, starts from a dark night of the soul, depicting Christ's 'veillée au jardin des oliviers et les baisers de Judas'. Since Christ and Judas are potentially present in each of us, the music starts from dichotomy: a long sustained A minor triad with added flat seventh haloes a stepwise-moving cantillation in parallel sevenths on woodwind, but is abruptly sundered by a 'très agité' interjection on brass, in savage dotted rhythm, with secundal dissonances and thrusting minor thirds. The tenors enter to enquire why we, Christ's disciples, had not the strength to watch with him, even for an hour. The tenor chant is pure Aeolian; but dichotomy is rife again when 'très violent' music in sharper tonalities heralds Judas. When the key shifts to G minor, the pounding minor thirds in the bass recall those that obsess *Les Carmélites*. But with a return to the original tempo the music enquires 'Quid dormitis?' calmly, over lulling seventh chords with piercing chromatics. Beginning around A flat, tonality shifts enharmonically through E major, and back to A with the Carmelitish minor thirds thudding glumly in the bass, only to be crowned by a triple-piano A major triad with added sixth and flat seventh—a cadence echoing the end of the convent chapel wake, after the Prioress's dire death in *Les Carmélites*. Similarly Judas's name, whispered on a low A by basses, may be an induction to transcendence.

But we wouldn't guess this from the movement that follows, for 'Judas mercator pessimus' is 'très violent et agité' music in a Stravinskian cross between C major and A minor, with savage syncopations harshly scored. Metrically, the piece is irregular and disrupted, with a force that again recalls *Oedipus Rex*. When the words refer to the 'agnus innocens' who seems to be, but isn't, Judas's victim, the vocal lines flow more smoothly around B minor, leading to a recapitulation of the Judas-music a tone higher. The setting of 'Christum Judaeis tradidit' returns to the furious minor thirds, depressing them to G minor, reinforced by blaring brass. A very slow coda sets the words 'Melius illi erat' to a piteous chromatic phrase centred on D, but fading on a dominant seventh of B flat. Out of this the original A minor triad with flat seventh distantly hums, while the basses, on low A, whisper the name Judas.

The next *répons* is for Calvary. Its opening juxtaposes a chromatically anguished monody, dominated by oboe, with funereal crotchets as marching bass, supporting quavers phrased in 'weeping' pairs. The quavers borrow one of Bach's basic musical images, while the monodic line could not have happened had Poulenc been entirely ignorant of Schoenberg (see Example 49). The same figures turn aggressive when the chorus takes up the

Example 49 *Sept répons des ténèbres*, p. 23, first line (voices only).

'tradidit' motif, modulating to seven-flatted A flat minor. But with the reference to Peter, a fallible betrayer who none the less loved God, the penitential import of the Agony in the Garden is manifest in a luminous modulation to F sharp major, mutated into urgent processional music as Christ is led before Caiphas. In the concluding section the radiant invocation to Peter is screwed up a semitone higher, to G major; but the movement ends back in the minor, with thirds and sixths grinding in the orchestra while the lower voices of the chorus mumble 'Jesum tradidit'.

A brief orchestral postlude droops through a diminished seventh of 'horrendous' F minor, to be snuffed out on the telescoped tonic-dominant chord that had been the source of the music's tension. The next *répons*, 'Caligaverunt oculi mei', erupts from the previous movement in that its initial theme is even more angular in Schoenbergian chromatics than had been the theme of 'Jesum tradidit'; the scoring is harsh, never mollifying the dissonance. But the final section, tracing a parallel between Christ's suffering and our destiny, is, though acute in harmony, quiet in dynamics, sparse in scoring, wide-flung in spacing. One might even think, in connection with this music, of expressionist Webern.

For the fifth *répons* Poulenc turns to the text he had so memorably used in the *Motets de pénitence*. His new version of 'Tenebrae factae sunt' makes several references to the early ones; not, one suspects, in conscious quotation, but because the momentous words had generated musical images that he could not repudiate. The treble soloist opens by intoning the text in pentatonic monody around B and E. The upper voices of the chorus, in the Aeolian mode on B, utter Jesus's cry 'at the ninth hour'; and are reinforced by the soloist and orchestra in a swaying triple pulse, modulating to E flat minor. When Christ 'bows his head' treble solo and choric altos are intimately a cappella. Jesus 'emisit spiritum' to the same whole-tone undulation as occurs in the 1938 setting and the a cappella coda recapitulates the early setting's cadence from what sounds like a dominant seventh of C to a B minor triad, though the F natural of the dominant seventh is again notated as E sharp.

The sixth *répons* metamorphoses darkness into light by relating the entombment of Christ to his Easter resurrection. The brazen-textured music is in white C major, though mystery is manifest when the open, Stravinskian textures change to vacillating chromatic triads on the words 'volventes lapidum ad ostium monumenti'. We end, for the magical seventh *répons*, with an 'Ecce, quomodo moritus justus' that merits the epithet of sublime. The pulse is 'calme' over a steady ostinato of G major triads in pizzicato quavers, though the key-note is not G but B (see Example 50). The regular pulse and scalic movement are taken up by the chorus, while the orchestra transmutes the arpeggiated ostinato into rocking octaves comparable with those in *Tel jour, telle nuit* and in the Prioress's death-scene. Here, however, fear is allayed by the unbroken momentum, and by the rondo-like recurrence of the main theme and its ostinato. When the words tell us that the regenerative power of the Lamb may conquer dissolution and the bare bone, the music is momentarily savage in dissonance. Even so, the pulse never falters; and treble solo pipes the main theme above the chorus, while the orchestral ostinato returns unsullied.

Example 50 *Sept répons des ténèbres*, p. 40, l. 1.

Calme, mais sans traîner ♩ = 50

In the coda, however, the ostinato becomes an oscillation of semitones between F sharp and G. In the depths of the orchestra the oscillation then growls between B and C natural, below harmonies that iron out into a dominant seventh of a Neapolitan C. In the last three bars B minor magically flowers into B major, the triad widely spread, pianissimo, and still with a blue flat seventh. If these final chords with flat seventh seem to have become a Poulenc cliché, we must remember that clichés may be profoundly meaningful; indeed, this may be why they *become* clichés. This one reminds us once more that God, unlike ourselves, goes on 'world without end'; for us the process of rebirth must be perennial. Although, for obvious reasons, the *Sept Répons* will never be as popular as the *Gloria*, it is probably Poulenc's greatest religious work. There is piquancy in the fact that Poulenc did not in this project fulfil his temporal obligations, since he failed to complete the score in time for the opening of the Lincoln Center. When *Sept Répons* received their première in 1963 it was not in the Lincoln Center but in the Avery Fisher Hall, and not under Bernstein but under Thomas Schippers, with the New York Philharmonic. And by then Poulenc himself was dead.

8
POULENC LE BONHOMME: LE CONSERVATISME ET L'ENFANCE

1. Piano Concerto (1949) and Sinfonietta (1947)

While *Sept Répons des ténèbres* stands with *Figure humaine* and *Dialogues des Carmélites* as the highest and deepest point in Poulenc's work, it would be inappropriate to end a survey of so hedonistic a composer with religious music. For our penultimate chapter we return to Poulenc 'le bonhomme', beginning with a reference to two works written around his fiftieth year as unabashedly entertaining contributions to the normal concert repertory. His Piano Concerto was composed in 1949, more or less contemporary with the *Stabat Mater*. It has, however, no truck with the painful self-communing of that liturgical work, being a conservative piece in a conservative French genre—a successor to the piano concertos of the 'petit seigneur', Saint-Saëns. Poulenc wrote it for himself to play on his second American tour, hoping to amuse big audiences in big halls. In this aim he succeeded—because, rather than in spite of, the paradox inherent in his casting the first movement of a light concerto in 'serious' C sharp minor, and incorporating within it a largo of considerable length and gravity. The rococo-Mozartian slow movement is also too beautiful to count as escape-music, while the rondo finale, though scherzoid in character, is in F sharp minor, *sub*-dominant to the original C sharp. Moreover it ends not with an applause-generating peroration, but in a puff of smoke.

Two years previously, in 1947, Poulenc had fulfilled a BBC commission for an orchestral work of symphonic scope. Although it is about the same length as a Haydn symphony, Poulenc was wise to call his piece Sinfonietta, for it approaches symphonic form more in the spirit of French ballet music than of Haydn or Mozart. The first movement offers the basic duality of a tight rhythmic motif in the minor, and flowing, lyrical tunes in the major. Even so, the movement proceeds kaleidoscopically; and although beautifully scored, it sounds *over*scored, and slightly outstays its welcome. Similarly the scherzo, ludic 'enfantine'-music harking back to *Les Biches*, sounds, without stage action, inflated. The slow movement, with woodwind scoring and rococo tunes that reanimate the fragrance of *Les Biches*, is the most effective because it admits to being French ballet music without dancers. One has to acknowledge, however that there is something forlorn about dance music without dancers, as there is about café music without a café.

2. Élégie *for Horn and Piano (1957)*; Sonate *for Flute and Piano (1957)*; Sonates *for Clarinet and Piano, and for Oboe and Piano (1962)*

It would seem that Poulenc knew what he was doing when he eschewed symphonic concert music. During his last decade he composed church music and operas, but no straight orchestral music—though for his own pleasure he embarked on a series of works for a wind instrument and piano, perhaps inspired by the set of six 'sonates' that Debussy planned in the last years of his life. Debussy had completed only three of these works at the time of his death; Poulenc too was defeated by the grim reaper, though it is improbable that his was a carefully planned project. He wrote the sonatas because he had always been partial to wind instruments, which are closely allied to the human voice, whereas 'nothing could be further from human breath than the stroke of a bow'. While he wrote effectively for strings in his theatre music, he didn't favour the string family in chamber music. In the 1940s he sketched out a string quartet, but abandoned it as 'disastrous' on hearing it played through by the Calvet Quartet (a few of the tunes, at the suggestion of Henri Sauguet, were salvaged for the Sinfonietta). Rostropovitch, after hearing *La Voix humaine* in 1960, wrote Poulenc a fan letter saying that on the evidence of that 'marvellous opera' Poulenc was 'the only one who could make a cello sing with a "human voice". I beg of you on behalf of cellists the world over to offer this gift to all musicians.' Poulenc resisted this appeal, probably because he had already written a cello and piano sonata in 1948, for Fournier and himself to play in their recitals. The piece had some success, but was not highly valued by its composer: who was ruthlessly dismissive of the violin and piano sonata he had composed in the same year, for Ginette Neveu and in memory of Lorca. 'Despite some delectable violinistic detail due entirely to Ginette Neveu,' he wrote, 'this sonata is clearly a failure, mainly because of its artificial pathos, and also, quite frankly, because I do not like the violin in the singular.' This judgement seems unnecessarily harsh; yet one has only to turn from the violin sonata to the opening of the sonata for flute and piano to sense the difference between struggle with a medium and its effortless realization. Although Poulenc seldom attempted sustained counterpoint and never assayed a symphonic movement in Beethovenian (or Shostakovitchean) style, he uses his collage techniques and his permutations on rondo and variation forms so adroitly that they not only succeed on a small scale, but may also be convincingly adapted to a large-scale structure like the *Gloria*, a sequence of brief movements like *Figure humaine*, and even to a full-sized opera like *Dialogues des Carmélites*. The small forms of the late wind and piano sonatas confirm this process by inversion, since they in turn borrow from the big works.

The cycle of sonatas seems to have been triggered by a one-movement piece that was not even called sonata. The *Élégie* for horn and piano is what it says it is: a memorial for the great Denis Brain. This strangely moving piece unexpectedly (and for Poulenc uniquely) opens with a 12-note row, with no tone repeated, magisterially chanted by unaccompanied horn, but brutally dismissed by a Stravinskian molto agitato passage in which both instruments utter aggressively false-related triads of C major and minor. The tension between Schoenberg and Stravinsky, polar opposites of twentieth-century music, seems to be adapted to Poulenc's own interior divisiveness; and the process is repeated, for the piano then sings the row as a unison melody, which is again dismissed by the agitato, now teetering between G major and minor, with acute major sevenths and minor ninths on the keyboard. In a 'très calme' bridge passage the horn's chromaticized cantilena evolves from, but is not serially related to, the row, and is accompanied by tingling major sevenths on piano. The main substance of the *Elégie* is a slow 3/4 aria for horn over swaying quavers in the piano's middle register, with a singing line in the bass. Both the spacious melody and the accompaniment are close to passages from the *Stabat Mater* and from *Dialogues des Carmélites*, the basic key being G minor. Carmelitish minor thirds pervade the texture as, reinforced by an eruption of the horn's stuttering in the agitato, climax is attained in heroic 'open' notes for horn. After culminating in fortissimo triads of E flat and C, both with flat sevenths, the cantillation unwinds into luminous four-part textures for the piano, into which the horn weaves references to the row. The *Elégie* ends, yet again, with a widespread pianissimo chord of C major, the horn sustaining the third while the piano touches in a flat seventh.

The enigmatic structure of this piece must surely have some allegorical, if not explicitly programmatic, intention. The ferocious agitato snarls like Death himself, who destroyed Denis Brain in a car accident, as he had slaughtered Pierre-Octave Ferroud in 1936. The 12-note row may be merely an instance of Francis trying himself out in a then-fashionable convention, as he certainly did in the *Thème varié* for piano of 1951. But it makes sense if the tone-row 'stands for' the immutable Will of God which, since the work is not serially constructed, has a merely arbitrary connection with human destiny. The horn-song is Poulenc's quasi-vocal response to God's all-too-mysterious way, in which we as mourners may join vicariously. It embraces many references to, and even quotations from, Poulenc's own past music: as do the final trio of sonatas, though these have no specific association with a death—or even with Death—apart from the fact that the last of them ends with a 'Déploration'.

Although these sonatas do not pretend to be great music, they leave us in no doubt that the composer who wrote *Dialogues des Carmélites* is in more than one sense behind them. An inkling of this is given in the directive Poulenc gives to the first movement of the flute and piano sonata, written in the same year (1957) as the horn *Élégie*. The piece is in 'purgatorial' E minor, and the directive of 'allegretto malinconico' proves appropriate, though there would seem to be more vivacity than melancholy in the flute's spring-like opening phrase: which kicks off with a broken triad of demisemiquavers around high E and declines in gentle chromatics to the G above middle C (see Example 51). The piano's left hand sustains a pedal E, while the right interweaves arpeggiated semiquavers. The conventional eight-bar phrase is answered by a four-bar phrase, beginning in C major but returning by way of a Neapolitan progression to B minor and then back to E for a further repetition of the opening clause. The modification entails a 'real' modulation to C major–minor, shifting to a half-close in A minor: in which key the main theme appears delicately decorated, the demisemiquavers floating airborne, like a bird.

Example 51   Sonata for flute and piano: first movement, p. 1, l. 1, and first bar of l. 2.

A counter-theme, though hardly a second subject, appears in F major, with the flute bouncing its arpeggios upward; the piano's broken arpeggios are now scherzoid, youthfully aware, in floating modulations and fluttery repeated notes, of evanescence. This prepares us for the return of the lyrical melody in dark F minor and E flat minor, before it drifts to A minor for a recapitulation of the main theme. The return of the ostensible 'first subject' in the wrong key is evidence that this is no aborted sonata form, but a subtle ternary structure. Five bars of transition, beginning with parallel $\frac{6}{3}$ chords in F sharp minor, relative of A *major*, lead to a middle section in slightly faster tempo. The flute's melody dips and soars, again bird-like but now distraught in the dotted rhythm pervasive in both *Les Carmélites* and *La Voix humaine*.

And when a da capo of the first section of the ternary form finally appears, it too is in the 'wrong' key of A instead of E minor. Yet although not orthodox, this subdominant recapitulation is right rather than wrong in that it mollifies the ecstasy, fused with strain and stress, that the middle section shares with the two operas, one produced just before the sonata was written, the other a year or so later. In any case unorthodox A minor turns into C major, which serves as a Neapolitan approach to B minor, dominant of E minor: in which tonic a 'true' recapitulation follows. Recapitulation is, however, an inadequate, even misleading term, for the reborn music involves enharmonic ambiguities that justify the 'malinconico' of the directive. Fragments of the first section's airborne melody intermingle with ecstatic spurtings of the middle theme. A coda to the coda is explicitly based on blue false relations between major and minor thirds.

Echoes of those Carmelite nuns haunt this vernal movement, as they do the succeeding Cantilena. Music for the New Prioress in *Dialogue des Carmélites* is directly recalled in the B flat minor canon and floating, stepwise-declining melody with which this slow movement opens. A more richly scored repeat of the phrase, accompanied by levelly reiterated quavers, modulates not to the dominant, but to A minor and G minor, and thence to more recondite keys. The exquisite theme remains pervasive, now combined with a more energetic, dotted-rhythmed melody referring back to the middle section of the first movement and to the painful ecstasies of the Carmelities, while also anticipating the anguished dotted-rhythmed motif in *La Voix humaine*. Frequent changes of key and of time signature give this section a restless, if not developmental, feeling, until a climax, in F sharp minor, revives the strenuous thrust of the 'bridge' passage in the first movement. A brief, six-bar recapitulation of the first theme resolves in a *tierce de Picardie*. This movement combines lyrical charm with a Carmelitish tragic pathos.

But the finale seems to be little-boy Poulenc reborn, presto giocoso in innocent A major. Poulenc's probably intuitive handling of tonality is again potent. A is the subdominant of E and in that sense lower, more relaxed; but A major is brighter than E minor, or even than the equivocal major–minor of the first movement. So this rondo balances between highlights and halflights, beginning with a café-concert tune in 2/4, based on a ta-tata rhythm of crotchets and quavers. The flute flickers, the piano bounces, in a helter-skelter gallop, as the rondo tune recurs in a plethora of keys. The episodes sometimes temper ebullience with lyricism, but may also hint at subterranean matters—especially in an episode built over a revolving 'cam' in the pianist's (sinister) left hand, above which the flute burbles references to the bird-like quiverings (and semiquaverings) of the first movement. These chatterings culminate in a long trill on high G, followed by an expectant silence: out of which emerges, *un*expectedly, a quotation from the dotted rhythmed theme of the first movement's middle, in its original key of F sharp minor. A breath-holding return of the revolving cam leads back, at the original delirious tempo, to the rondo tune, in its initial A major. The coda toys with fragments of the multifarious material of the whole sonata, with a mastery of interconnectedness that reminds us that Poulenc, if a master of 'light' music, also composed two operas and several religious works that have tragic potential.

Despite the sonata's spontaneity, the subtlety of its art is evident in its tonal plan: a first movement centred on an ambiguous E minor, a slow movement *radiantly* in dark B flat minor, and a finale not in heavenly E major, which would be going *too* far, but in the major of the subdominant A, a key of youth and hope. If the companion sonatas for a wind instrument with piano are darker pieces than the flute sonata, this is not so much because, written in the last year of the composer's life, they convey intimations of mortality as because clarinet and oboe are more plangently expressive instruments than flute, and a good composer is responsive to an instrument's nature and potential.

The first movement of the clarinet sonata is headed 'Allegro tristamente', an ambiguous directive that complements the 'allegretto malinconico' of the flute sonata's first movement. As befits the instrument, the clarinet sonata is fiercer than the flute work—life-asserting, yet a shade desperate. Into a briefly wild introduction the clarinet spatters fragmented semiquavers, punctuated by dissonances on piano. Tonality has not been clearly established when the introduction ends with a tremolando on (sounding) E and G on clarinet and a chromaticized dominant of C on piano. C is established as the basic key of the allegro proper, which opens with rocking octaves similar to, even quoted from, those in *Tel jour, telle nuit* and in *Dialogues des Carmélites*. They may again be Time's clock, ticking beneath a clarinet melody that arches through a C major arpeggio and declines in a tail of semiquavers.

After modulating to G minor, the clarinet stimulates its melodic arch with a dotted rhythm. The transformed theme, its chromaticized accompaniment, and the upward-sweeping scales are close to the Agnus of the *Gloria* Poulenc had recently composed, and carry similar religious overtones. Eventually, the clarinet demolishes songful serenity with a return of the fragmentary interjections of the introduction.

Far from leading to development, this causes breakdown, hopefully redeemed by a contrasted middle section, 'très calme et très doux' in 3/4. The tonality is A flat major–minor, and the clarinet melody describes a gentle arch. Shifting up a tone to B flat minor, the figuration becomes rocking quaver chords, above which the clarinet spurts dotted-rhythmed themes that come near to quoting the Domine Deus and Agnus of the *Gloria* (see Example 52).

Example 52   Sonata for clarinet and piano: first movement, p. 8, l. 3, omitting first bar.

This marriage of anguish and aspiration subsides when the key sinks to A minor and G minor, the dynamics now soft, and with the clarinet's eruptions immediately balanced by descents. A da capo of the allegro is, as usual, truncated, and also deprived of tension because the piano's bass is now a censer-like swaying between G major thirds. This ostinato does not swing to rest, for after a brief silence the dotted rhythm returns impudently on piano, interspersed with clarinet references to the introduction. The final cadence is unexpectedly a triad of B minor, through which the clarinet murmurs tremolando thirds.

The Romanza is not only darker, but also more exotic. The clarinet opens with an unaccompanied cantillation of D, F sharp, B flat, and E flat, faintly liturgical but also folk-like. Accompanied by a chromaticized G minor chord on piano, the clarinet sweeps away the incantatory motif with quasi-Moorish arabesques, before moving into a melody in slow triple time, garlanded with dotted-rhythmed roulades. The piano part, at first softly syncopated, settles into level quavers over a singing bass. With a modulation to B minor the piano's right hand inverts the clarinet's whirlingly decorated melody, creating music again close to the Agnus of the *Gloria*. This intimate Romanza has justified its link with the grand Christian theme: especially when the coda modulates from A flat minor back to G minor and C minor. The moment when the C minor triad clears to C major is not the less magical because Poulenc had often used it. The quasi-Moorish arabesques stridently return on high clarinet, as 'out of *this* world' as the yell of a peacock (see Example 53).

The finale lives up to its directive of 'Allegro con fuoco', its overt key now being the C major the first movement had toyed with. The piano hammers chords in quavers, above which the clarinet explosively chirrups. There is a harshness in the music that should be reflected in the clarinet's tone—more like a peasant-pipe than a concert-clarinet. The second theme refers back to the bridge theme from the first movement but, fused with the main theme, merges into a more lyrical tune in A flat minor. For Poulenc, this movement comes fairly close to sonata form: after a transitional passage (based on the lilting quaver bass of the first movement) the lyrical melody takes off in what almost amounts to a development. It ranges through many keys, climaxing over a pedal point on the basic tonic C. The piano's accompanying chords are syncopated, while the clarinet flirts with the whirring

Example 53 Sonata for clarinet and piano: romanza, p. 15, l. 3.

semiquavers of the first theme, and with arabesques that relate to the 'Moorish' cantillation of the first movement. A sonata-style recapitulation, not subject to Poulenc's usual truncation, allows scope for both the savage first subject and the slow second tune. A fierce coda is metrically disrupted, with an effect more alarming than comic, though it may induce a nervous titter. The percussive piano sonority in the last five bars is wild peasant-music, as is the clarinet's ultimate screech. In a sense Poulenc has come full circle. His boyhood clarinet pieces had been stimulated by Stravinsky's Russian child-peasants; at the end of his life these piping peasants are sun-baked, in his beloved Morvan.

The oboe and piano sonata has a remote link with Russian peasants in being dedicated to the memory of Prokofiev. Its gravity is, however, elegiac rather than savage, and its wildness is rooted in la Belle France. The first movement is explicitly called 'Elégie'. Beginning with a distant, unaccompanied cantillation on oboe, it becomes an aria in G major, 'paisiblement' over a padding bass starting from oscillating thirds in G. The oboe melody noodles around the G above middle C, aspires upwards, and shifts, with the ostinato bass, to B minor. The piano insinuates the oboe's melody into its middle range, and extends its tailpiece towards E flat major. But the movement never threatens to become a sonata form; after cadencing from E flat to B flat, Poulenc moves into a middle section in which quaver arpeggios accompany a new tune in dotted rhythm. This has no whiff of the heroic, being an 'enfantine' more gaminish, even gypsy-like, in spirit than wide-eyed; it may have been inspired by the slightly sinister if child-like theme in Debussy's orchestral *Gigues*. Again, experience proves malleable; tonality shifts to D major–minor, and thence to B flat minor with the *Gigues*-like ludic tune marrying its wildness to the heroic intensities of the *Gloria*'s Agnus Dei, and to several agonized passages from *La Voix humaine* (see Example 54). Out of these arabesques the oboe winds back to its first 'noodling' theme, over its original G major ostinato. The da capo is shortened, to lead into a lyrical peroration over telescoped chords of G major and B minor, which had proved so potent at the end of the *Gloria*. But the coda is neither consummatory nor resolved. The dotted rhythm motif reappears, fiercely, on oboe, while the piano transmutes its 'paisiblement' major thirds into minor thirds in syncopation. The oboe's distant cry of the major third is effaced by glassy piano chords over a tonic pedal.

The scherzo has no key signature but is basically in B flat minor, with many of the implications that key has in *Dialogues des Carmélites*. Thinly scored for piano, it flickers in fast jig-time, exploiting the oboe's facility in rapid repeated notes, as well as its aptitude for song. In the middle there is a sudden explosion of the eruptive motif from the middle of the first movement, and also pervasive in the two late operas. This stimulates rather than staunches momentum, until the flow stops abruptly on a dominant of D minor. The tempo slows to half time for a ripely expansive trio beginning in D major, its theme evolved from the rising semiquaver motif of the first movement. Through wide-ranging modulations the heartfelt, heart-easing music suggests a Parisian Rachmaninov, more surprising in this context than it is in the comparable passages in the conservative Piano Concerto. Still, the

Example 54 Sonata for oboe and piano: first movement, p. 5, l. 1, bars 2-3, and l. 2, bar 1.

elegiac tone accords with a retrospective sonata, especially when, in the F major resolution, a syncopated pedal note prods the music back to B flat and to a shortened, but still fierce, da capo of the scherzo. The minor thirds of the final bar, marked 'rude', are deathly, though without the tragic implications of the Carmelites' minor thirds.

The last movement, 'Déploration', is a lament on or by a tomb—an elegy not only for dead Prokofiev and dying Poulenc, but also for la Belle France, since the convention pays deference to the 'déplorations' that early French composers like Josquin and

Ockeghem were wont to write for their revered masters. The tempo is triple and 'très calme'; the tonality is very dark A flat minor, though Poulenc doesn't write its seven flats into a key signature, as he did in 'Cé', his wartime lament for 'ma France délaissée'. The piano prelude is in three severely modal parts; the oboe wails its lament over a sustained chord of A flat minor with flat seventh. The melody is Dorian on A flat, the piano chord being unchanged until it shifts to C minor, through which the oboe, suddenly double-forte, howls at the bottom of its register. The lament is repeated very softly, and expands into embryonic aria, with the piano eliding chords of G major and B minor, as at the end of the *Gloria*. A chromatic wriggle in the bass twists back to A flat minor, the piano murmuring a monotone of tonic chords over an ostinato of major sevenths. Aloft, the oboe recalls both the 'noodling' theme and the dotted-rhythmed motif of the first movement.

A heroic climax is attained in white-note (Aeolian) A minor; this subsides back to A flat as the oboe recollects the 'enfantine' in dotted rhythm from the first movement, and the piano takes it up in F minor. All these thematic cross-references give the piece a unity, an interrelationship between parts and whole, which validates its being called a sonata though none of its movements is in sonata form. The coda starts from the F minor chord with added major seventh, supporting the oboe's initial cantillation. But the piano wafts back, 'triste et morne' like the Carmelites in prison, to A flat minor, while the oboe spins chromatic undulations around the note E flat—an impersonal, even universalized, mutation of the oboe's tune in the first movement.

At this point the piano insinuates through its calmly ticking A flat minor thirds a motif floating between C natural, E flat, and F flat. The C naturals clash in false relation with the C flats of the A flat minor thirds, while we hear the C, E flat, and F flat motif as blue notes in C, since on an equal-tempered piano F flat and E natural are identical (see Example 55). The effect, though pathetic, is also grand—almost as purgatorial as the comparable passages in the final scene of *Dialogues des Carmélites*. The last sounds we hear are a sepulchral chord of A flat minor with an added *major* seventh, allowed to vibrate beneath the oboe's forlornly sustained E flat. This sonata may be a small work lasting a mere thirteen minutes; but it embraces a lifetime's experience, from the capers of childhood, to the passions and perils of

Example 55 Sonata for oboe and piano, 'Déploration', p. 22, ll. 3 and 4.

adolescence, to the tensions between positive and negative impulses typical of maturity, to the desolations and declensions of old age. The word experience—from the Latin *ex periculo*—means from or out of peril. Humane Poulenc is a comforter who heals our contrarieties often with good humour, but sometimes with a tragic pathos that helps us to bear our personal agony impersonally. If this seems a lot to claim for a brief oboe sonata, we may find justification in the many relationships we have traced between this modest opus ultimum and the major creations of Poulenc's life.

3. The Last Song-Cycle: La Courte Paille (1960)

One other small, indeed tiny, work from Poulenc's opera ultima demands attention: his last contribution to the genre in which he thought himself most expert, the song-cycle. This fits the pattern we have discerned in the music of his last years, for although *La Courte Paille* is often performed in recitals, its origins were as 'performance music' in a very practical sense. Francis wrote the songs for Denise Duval to sing to her young son: for *La Courte Paille* sets seven nonsense verses for children by Maurice Carême, thereby linking Poulenc's life-long obsession with childhood to his current concern with performance music, in the context of daily life. We are told that Poulenc's well-known and much-loved *L'Histoire de Babar l'Éléphant* was improvised at the piano by Francis to a reading of the tale, at the request of a small niece. The incident happened in 1940, though Poulenc didn't formally revise and publish the piece until 1945. Although ephemeral 'fun-music' for a little girl, for the most part exploiting 'Mickey Mouse' techniques illustrative of the words, the music touches the heart, as well as tickling the funny-bone. The prologue and epilogue—respectively evoking a lullaby for the baby Babar and the serenity of the jungle night after the high jinks of his wedding—are exquisite Poulenc pianism, anticipatory of the idiom of the children's songs that are his final song-cycle. Poulenc, pleased with these songs, thought them 'very poetic and whimsical', as well as meticulous as to their prosody.

Interestingly enough, the first number, 'Le Sommeil', is neither nonsensical nor especially childish, for the mother is singing to a child who is perhaps sick, certainly unable to sleep cosily. This reminds us of the point made in reference to the slightly sinister,

Gigues-like 'enfantine' in the oboe sonata; Poulenc's children may be at once innocent and cruel, since they are not sentimentalized. In this song we see the child through his mother's eyes and mind, as she croons her lullaby to a syllabic vocal line based on stepwise movement and basic fourths and fifths. The key is C major, the tempo 'très calme', the rhythm a lulling of four crotchets a bar. Piano syncopations and occasional chromatics in the vocal line suggest the child's restlessness. In the last clause the parallel triads become $^6_4$ chords over a dominant pedal, and the song ends on an unresolved dominant seventh because mother isn't sure whether her child is ready to greet the new day's sun, his own exploring fingers, the morning milk, the daily bread. This is not so much a reference to a specific, possibly sick, child as a general comment on the human condition: out of 'le sommeil' are born our dreams and nightmares.

This is evident in the sequence of small songs which, although more 'poetic and whimsical' than scary, are bubblings from the boy's sub- or pre-consciousness. 'Quelle aventure' describes a flea driving a carriage with a miniscule elephant in it. It is the grotesque absurdity that delights and slightly alarms the child, as flickering chromatic quavers, 'très vite et rhythmé', are irradiated by sequential sevenths on the piano. Excitement builds as the scene grows more surreal, the flea-driven carriage careering madly on while the tiny elephant 'absentmindedly sucks a pot of jam'. The headlong pace never flags until the song stops abruptly when the child, coming down to earth, wonders how *on* earth he'll convince Mama that such things happen. This is a last-minute recollection of Poulenc's Nogent music. He also remarked that his Maurice Carême songs reminded him of *Les Mamelles de Tirésias*, a favourite piece because so spontaneously an overflow of his child-like heart.

Poulenc asks for a long silence before the next number which, 'calme et languide' in flowing quavers in 9/8 or 12/8, describes a Fairy Queen who regally bows as she presides over a court of lovers, including the young dead. The melody floats up and down the Aeolian mode on E for its first phrase, then aspires upwards like a wave of the courtly hand (see Example 56). The piano pulses in quavers, with a singing bass of dotted crotchets, pointing tender harmonies and simple modulations to and from B minor. In the final *tierce de Picardie* the Queen's hoar-frost castle shines 'aux doux vitraux de lune'. This little song rivals Ravel's fairy princesses music.

Example 56 *La Courte Paille*, no. 3, p. 6, first five bars.

The presence of the dead in the Queen's court may bear on the song's poignancy; similarly, there is danger within the nonsense of 'Ba, Be, Bi, Bo, Bu', in which the tempo is 'follement vite', while the wild key is E flat minor, and the piano writing 'terriblement sec'. But if this Puss in Boots starts as tigerishly fearsome, he becomes benign in sequential sevenths when, laughing at his own antics, he returns to his castle. The final revelation of his identity is in parallel $^6_4$ chords over a cascading chromatic bass, 'surtout sans ralentir': an effect at once comic and scary, in the way children relish. We need to take a breath before the next song, which seems as guileless as Eden, which none the less nurtured a serpent. The tune of 'Les Anges musiciens' is as simple as a nursery ditty, doubled by piano and haloed by lulling quavers in thirds. When we are told that it's always Mozart the angels sing it is Poulenc who is speaking, and who makes the vocal intervals expand into sixths, sweetly rocking in D major, while the piano glows in its internal pedal notes. Initially, the key had been B flat, which is the tonality of Mozart's last Piano Concerto, the finale of which is based on a real children's song. The middle section is in D major; the piano postlude slides to E minor but ceases rather than concludes on a chord of E major with blue flat seventh. Heaven would seem to be a dream endemic not only to children, but also to mothers and composing uncles, 'an berceau'.

A return, or regression, to real childhood nonsense occurs in the song about a carafe that wants a baby carafe, just as a giraffe expects, and is entitled, to have a baby giraffe. This is an idiot rhyming game that catches the essence of childhood humour—as does Poulenc's music, 'très sec' in music-hall rhythms, fleetingly caressed by lyricism. The music renders the deliciously absurd parallels between the behaviour of giraffes and carafes, adult and juvenile, farcical yet still 'poetic and whimsical'. Tonality is crazily free, but the last verse settles for F sharp major–minor, sometimes enharmonically notated.

Poulenc asks for another long pause before the final song, 'Lune d'avril', which is an epilogue and retrospect. It returns to the C major and chromaticized chord sequence of the first song, with the same lullingly syncopated rhythm. Poulenc's directive is 'très lent et irréal', and the lovely words are sur-real in describing how the April moon irradiates a peach tree with a saffron heart, a laughing fish, a bird who awakens the dead, a 'pays où il fait joie, où il fait clair'. What safeguards the verse and music from a

Example 57 *La Courte Paille*, no. 7, p. 16, ll. 2 and 3.

debilitating softness is their magic and mystery which, in Blakean terms, 'reconcile the opposites', making the cycle a perfect curtain to Poulenc's song-writing. The final consummatory passage is almost identical with passages commented on in *Tel jour, telle nuit, Dialogues des Carmélites, Gloria,* and *Sept Répons des ténèbres* (see Example 57). The piano's postlude pares to the essence the chords that had introduced the preludial song, 'Le Sommeil'. The syncopated pedal note rests on middle C, 'immuablement dans le même tempo'. The final chord, glowing with a flat seventh, suspends the child in time, waiting for ensuing life—and for inevitable death.

POSTLUDE

Un honnête homme: Poulenc, le passé, et l'avenir

Looking back on Poulenc and his music, we recognize that we value him because, as 'un homme moyen sensuel', he like most of us was imbued with basic human strengths and weaknesses. In his adolescent works he, like his master Satie, was engaged in small acts of transcendence that had the wide-eyed and open-eared wonder of a child; in his middle years he made a conservative music that discovered, as any true artist must, new truths within accredited conventions—as is evident in, for instance, his handling of the traditional 'meanings' of tonal relationships. In his last decade transcendence in the specifically religious sense was the theme of his major opera and of the *Stabat Mater*, the *Gloria*, and the *Sept Répons des ténèbres*, next to the opera his most substantial pieces. No wonder he wrote in a letter to Simone Girard that although he was 'not intoxicated with the idea of being a Grrrrand Musician, it none the less exasperates me to be thought of by so many people as nothing more than a "petit maître érotique"'.

The durability of his works has by this date made such a view obsolete, and has justified the esteem accorded him by so many distinguished people. Many tributes to him have been quoted in the course of this book. No one can condescend to a composer of whom Stravinsky remarked: 'You are truly *good*, and that is what I find again and again and again in your music.' Even as late as 1946, when his own compositional path had deviated far from that of his Parisian years, the American Stravinsky had not abated his 'warm regard for what you are doing', and was requesting Francis to 'send me some of your own music; you know what loyal and tender feelings I have always had for your bewitching muse'. The 'goodness' of Poulenc and his music seems to have been therapeutic in effect. Jean Cocteau, the tormented if hedonistic companion of Poulenc's youth, went so far as to say, in 1924, that 'your works are the only things that keep me going, and give me the curiosity to carry on living'. A decade later Manuel de Falla confessed that 'your music brings me precious relief. How I loved your concerto [for two pianos and orchestra], with its beautiful

179

directness of expression and the lively sympathy that endows your music so admirably and exceptionally.'

Clearly, Poulenc was a composer for whom music was a friendly act. Many were grateful for the wisdom he offered, as is evident in the beautiful letter he wrote in 1937 to the singer Suzanne Peignot, advising her on her professional career:

Think about all this and you will see that everything I am telling you is absolutely right. What I am suggesting [that she should join the Nadia Boulanger Singers] is so attractive, lively, and appealing, and would take you out of yourself so well that if I were you I would jump at the opportunity. Otherwise, continue making your hats, have your picture in *Vogue*, and go on living a life that I do not believe is right for you. You have better things to do. Only a well-regimented Suzanne will *progress*, will become a star again, and make us forget the poor little wounded bird. So there you have it.

Few could take offence at so affectionate a reprimand; and it is worth noting, since the essence of friendship is that it must work in both directions, that Poulenc could accept criticism himself. Pierre Bernac, his longest and dearest friend as well as his revered professional colleague, was an arbiter in matters moral, aesthetic, and spiritual. He had the right to reprove Francis when he was in the depths of his Lucien-trauma, writing in November 1954:

Unfortunately, through your lack of moral virility you have worn down the affection of this loyal but not very interesting boy. I am sorry for you if you really love him as much as you think you do, something of which I am not entirely sure. You loved the character you wanted him to play, at your side. If you had really loved him, you would have loved him for himself, and not for yourself. Be that as it may, the situation is now quite unequivocal. . . . Face the reality plainly and squarely, and put up with it. You are neither the first nor the last to suffer a broken heart. It is too convenient to put everything down to illness. Your inclination to let yourself go does not date from that date. What is more, there is human dignity to be preserved. I suffer so much to see you losing it so completely in the eyes of everyone, not only your friends. Francis Poulenc, even on the human plane, is surely greater than this. Have no doubt that this feebleness will eventually make itself felt in your art. Life is not a matter of easy solutions. . . . If you think that you cannot react like a man—and I myself am certain that you can—then I must ask you to tell me now, for in that case we would do better to cancel the tour.

Bernac was justified in his confidence, for Poulenc survived, as did his art; and if we see that marvellous letter as complementary to Poulenc's letter to Suzanne Peignot, we'll better understand how Poulenc's strength and weakness together endear him to us.

A double man is likely to be emotionally as well as sexually volatile. Being French, Poulenc did not suffer from hang-ups about his sexuality such as British Britten laboured under, but he was subject to emotional extremes. When he was high he was very, very high, but when he was low he was horrid; and his moments of near-suicidal despair—'full of moss and melancholy'—were occasioned as much by failures of confidence in his creativity as by his love affairs, whether they were agonizing traumas like the relationship with Lucien, or whether they were ephemeral like the usually low-class youths who fleetingly tickled his fancy. Yet everyone forgave him his peccadilloes, and testified to the generosity of his heart. It was the formidable Wanda Landowska who wrote a postcard addressed to 'Mon Francis que j'aime', thanking him for 'your radiant goodness, the way you listen . . . a source of happiness'. Paul Eluard himself, to whom Poulenc acknowledged that he owed so much, reciprocated that homage when he wrote: 'Thank you for your clear, intelligent, intelligible music.'

Poulenc's self-assessment, except in rare moments of euphoria, was modest. In a reply to Bernac's letter of reproof quoted above he confessed that

too much introspection has been gnawing away at me for months. My consuming love for Lucien, which far from abating only seems to grow more intense, made me fall into a blind panic that was not helped at all by worries about my liver! My work is the only thing that will pull me out of this and in that respect I have not lost my touch. In an extraordinary moment of emotion and turmoil the final moments of *Les Carmélites* came to me, Blanche's arrival and her march to the scaffold. Looking at this music coldly, I honestly believe that it is overwhelming in its simplicity, in its resignation and . . . in its peace.

This physician, whose music could heal others, could indeed heal himself, and the interdependence of healer and healed contributes to his potent appeal. 'Although every now and again I ask myself why I continue to compose, and for whom', Poulenc wrote to his biographer Henri Hell in March 1961, 'there are several of my old things that continue to be played, and what counts is not what is played, but what is played again and again. After all, my music is not all that bad. In any case I think that in the future I will be played more often than Barraqué or Pousseur.' He will, and indeed is.

Arthur Honegger, a founder-member of Les Six who followed paths remote from Poulenc's, wrote in 1954 that separation had

only heightened the affection I have for you as a loyal friend, and the admiration I have for you as a musician, as a born creator of music, which sets you apart from so many others. In the midst of the modes, the systems, the methods that the incompetent have tried to impose you have remained true to yourself with a rare courage that commands respect.

Charles Koechlin, the instructor of Poulenc's youth, wrote in similar vein in 1945, remarking that 'there is a Poulenc style, and you know how to be, sincerely and simply, *yourself.* If I don't like everything in that last collection of songs, I conclude with pleasure that I always know they are by Poulenc, and that they are above all *music.*' When he adds that 'the intense and noble emotion of "Cé" breathes the very soul of our wounded fatherland' he touches on the transcendent qualities that—in *Quatre Motets pour un temps de pénitence, Figure humaine, Dialogues des Carmélites, Gloria, Sept Répons des ténèbres*, and possibly in *La Voix humaine* and even the little oboe sonata—make Poulenc momentarily a great composer. For the rest, he makes music that enhances our lives. He deserves our gratitude which, loving him, we are unlikely to withhold.

INDEX OF WORKS

183

GENERAL INDEX